THE KAZAKSTANI ECONOMY

UNIVERSITY OF READING EUROPEAN AND
INTERNATIONAL STUDIES

General Editor: Christoph Bluth

This series includes books which discuss some of the major contemporary
European and international issues from a comparative perspective.
National experiences with a relevance for broader European and
international issues are also covered by this series.

The collection is interdisciplinary in nature with the aim of bringing
together studies that emphasise the role of political, economic, historical
and cultural factors in shaping the course of international co-operation and
international conflicts, particularly from the point of view of Europe and
its relations with the rest of the world.

The influence of the processes of European integration (economic,
political, cultural) on both Europe and the rest of the world, as well as the
impact on Europe of global integration processes and non-European
integration schemes are some of the themes that run through the volumes
included in the series.

The Kazakstani Economy

Independence and Transition

Yelena Kalyuzhnova
*Co-ordinator of the Centre for Euro-Asian Studies,
Research Fellow at the Graduate School of
European and International Studies,
and Honorary Research Fellow
Department of Economics
University of Reading*

UNIVERSITY OF READING EUROPEAN
AND INTERNATIONAL STUDIES

The Centre for
Euro-Asian Studies

First published in Great Britain 1998 by
MACMILLAN PRESS LTD
Houndmills, Basingstoke, Hampshire RG21 6XS and London
Companies and representatives throughout the world

A catalogue record for this book is available from the British Library.

ISBN 0–333–69123–7

First published in the United States of America 1998 by
ST. MARTIN'S PRESS, INC.,
Scholarly and Reference Division,
175 Fifth Avenue, New York, N.Y. 10010

ISBN 0–312–21223–2

Library of Congress Cataloging-in-Publication Data
Kalyuzhnova, Yelena.
Kazakstani economy : independence and transition / Yelena
Kalyuzhnova.
p. cm.
Includes bibliographical references (p.   ) and index.
ISBN 0–312–21223–2 (cloth)
1. Kazakstan—Economic conditions—1991–   2. Kazakstan—Economic
conditions.   I. Title.
HC420.5.K35 1997
330.95845—dc21   97–38362
                                                                               CIP

This book is printed on paper suitable for recycling and made from fully managed and
sustained forest sources.

10   9   8   7   6   5   4   3   2   1
07   06   05   04   03   02   01   00   99   98

Printed and bound in Great Britain by
Antony Rowe Ltd, Chippenham, Wiltshire

For Andrei

Contents

List of Tables, Boxes and Figures

List of Tables

List of Boxes

List of Maps

List of Figures

Preface

I have chosen for my consideration and analysis one of the most interesting countries amongst the newly independent states – Kazakstan. The current economic conditions in Kazakstan are the result of a long process, which began in the years of the USSR.

I have been studying the Kazakstani economy for over ten years. My work in Kazakstan since 1989 and later my three years of research in Great Britain have helped me to understand the process of economic transformation. This book is concerned with the economic development of Kazakstan, the main purpose of which is to provide the reader with the 'real picture' of what is happening in the Kazakstani economic sphere at present. I do not pretend to be a 'transitologist' and I do not attempt to apply any transition theory to Kazakstan. However, I am convinced that theoretical conclusions can be drawn from the Kazakstani experience of transition.

I cannot say that this book is written from a purely academic point of view. I lived in Kazakstan for more than twenty years, and therefore this work is also the outcome of personal involvement. I cannot separate myself from this country, and of course I also feel all the sorrows and very heavy pain for the future of Kazakstan. I want the transition in Kazakstan to be successful, and the people of this country to obtain a valuable and rewarding style of life.

Let me make several methodological notes. I have approached my discussion in a chronological fashion, and attempted to analyse events, effects and economic development conceptually. The book is divided into four parts, the first dealing with the last years of the planned economy in Kazakstan. The second explores the beginning of national sovereignty, the introduction of the new national currency and the first steps by the Kazakstani government on a course of reform. The third part covers the most important elements of economic changes: privatisation and industrial transformation. The concluding part gives a view of the methods of reforms in different sectors of the economy: the oil and gas industry, agricultural sector, banking system, and foreign economic activity. The final analysis is upon the socio-economic implication of transition.

For purposes of continuity, the terms 'USSR', 'Soviet' and 'Union' are interchangeable throughout the text. Original statistics from Kazakstan which were available to me have been used instead of those from international agencies, which themselves are based indirectly on original sta-tistics which are made available from official sources. To maintain confidentiality of the unofficial sources, they are referred to in the text as 'source A', 'source B' etc.

The book is aimed at readers who are interested in country development: businessmen who are doing business in Kazakstan; investors; the general public wanting an approach to Kazakstani development. It could be used as a text for university economic courses such as *Development beyond Central Planning*. It does not presume to cover all aspects of transition, and is really a case study of present-day Kazakstan. Of course the story continues and remains open-ended.

* * *

Many people assisted me in the course of the preparation of this book, some of whom I cannot name for political reasons.

I would have been unable to write this book without the strong support of my friends and colleagues. Kanat Berentayev has been a constant source of inspiration and ideas for more than ten years. I am very grateful to Arustan Yesentugelov for sharing his thoughts with me and for his encouragement. I would like to thank Janos Kornai for his important recommendations which I received in the initial stages of writing my book. I had the tremendous privilege of being appointed by the University of Reading (UK) as the Co-ordinator of the Centre for Euro-Asian Studies at the Graduate School of European and International Studies (1996), and this gave me the inestimable advantage of working with a team of researchers such as Paul Mosley, Yurii Shokamanov, Inna Shvedyuk, George Tridimas, Leonid Yanovskiy, Terry Jackson and Vassillii Zakshevskii. With the support of Timothy Ash (The Economist Intelligence Unit) I finalised my 'western' approach. Several friends agreed to read preliminary drafts of the book and have made valuable comments. In this regard I am particularly grateful to Mark Casson, Michael Kaser, Richard Pomfret, and Sir Derek Thomas for their time, attention and patience. I would also like to thank Linda Auld of Macmillan Press for her copy-editing

I would especially like to thank Christoph Bluth, who did everything to help the publication of this book from the very beginning (the original concept to write such a book), until the publication. I am therefore very obliged to him for his research support, and for providing the opportunities to revisit Kazakstan several times during the writing of this book.

I am immensely grateful to Nicholas Tucker (the Administrator of the Centre for Euro-Asian Studies), my PhD student, for all the tremendous contributions which he made to this book, and for his support and help during all the stages of writing. Our work together was fraught but fruitful.

I would never have done such work without the love and support of my husband Andrei, who devoted all his time to me.

Yelena Kalyuzhnova
Reading, UK

I

The Last Years of the Planned Economy: Kazak Soviet Socialist Republic

1 The Kazak Soviet Socialist Republic in the USSR

The collapse of the communist states and the relinquishing of communist ideologies has resulted in the Commonwealth of Independent States (CIS) searching for new relationships between the state and the market. Central planning failed to achieve the economic and social developments expected of it, and the market economy is viewed by many as the answer to the perceived failures of socialism. Although the ending of political control by the communist parties was abrupt, the manner in which economies have reacted and adjusted to the changes has varied significantly. The balance between adopting market oriented reforms and formally relinquishing socialism has been uneven and, in some instances, paradoxical. It is becoming increasingly evident that the experiences under central planning and the outcome of reforms are going to be mixed. The types of economic strategies and planning introduced in the different economies and the relations to the Soviet Union have vitally influenced the pattern of development in subsequent years.

The new orthodoxy that underlies the economic reforms being introduced in the ex-socialist economies places a much greater emphasis on the role of the market mechanism in the allocation of resources. The processes of economic, political, social and institutional change that the CIS economies are experiencing at the current time do not display enough similarity to permit a common description of the process of change. Differences with respect to historical background, contemporary economic and political structures, levels of development and degrees of structural change, are significant. Therefore the following will examine the economic background of the newly independent state – Kazakstan.

THE SOVIET ERA: A PERIOD OF ESTABLISHMENT

The Kazak Soviet Socialist Republic (Kaz SSR) was the second largest republic (in terms of area) of the Soviet Union after Russia, with a population of 17 million living on 2.7 million square kilometres of land-locked territory, located in South Asia, between Russia, Uzbekistan and China. (See Map 1.1; Table 1.1; Box 1.1.) The Kazak people constitute a minority

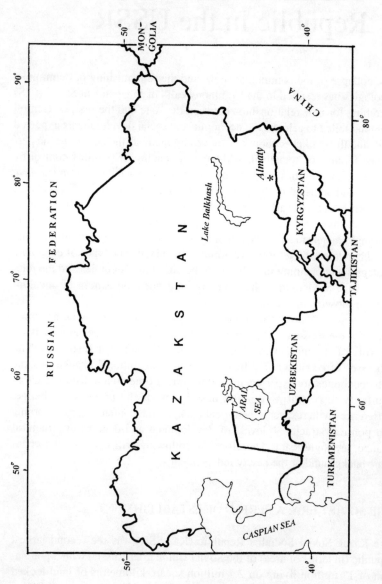

Map 1.1 Kazakstan and neighbouring countries

Table 1.1   Key Facts, 1990

Area (thousands of sq. km)	Population (millions)	Ethnic composition (%)	State language	Capital
2 717.3	16.793	41.0 Kazakh; 37.8 Russian; 5.8 German; 10.0 others	Kazak	Almaty

Source: State Statistical Committee of the Kaz SSR.

Box 1.1   Kazakstan short historical review

Formed from many different but related tribes, the Kazaks had pastoral nomadism as the prevalent economic activity up to the twentieth century. 'From the fifth to eighteenth centuries the nomadic tribe remained predominant, often with an economic, social and political elite composed of tribal leaders, chiefs and khans.' (Wieczynski, 1980: 81). In the eighteenth century, with the Russian Empire bordering on the lands of the Kazaks, the process of Russian influence and encroachment began. Russian influence on the Kazaks took place in all aspects of their living, and Russian settlers stimulated farming in the eighteenth century. Nomadic life decreased somewhat and a lot of people adopted a settled way of life. The Russian Government sent large numbers of Russian peasants to the Kazak territory to ease congestion on the land in the early twentieth century. 'Other Russians came to the cities, causing an increase in size and an expansion of commercial and cultural activities.' (Wieczynski, 1980: 82). Industries were developed for domestic consumption and external trade, particularly with Russia.

During the Soviet regime Kazakstan became a Soviet Republic. The culture and way of life of the Kazaks changed dramatically in the beginning of the twentieth century. The percentage of the agricultural population collectivised was 7.4 per cent in 1929, and 95 per cent in 1933 (Olcott, 1995) which drastically altered the life-style of the previously nomadic population. But the consequence of 'quick industrialisation and collectivisation' would be demonstrated later in the 1990s when the country announced its independence. '"Development" meant the development of raw material or food supplies or of trading profits. The colonial power was primarily interested in supplies and profits, not in the development of the natives, and this meant it was primarily interested in the colony's exports and not in its internal market'. (Schumacher, 1993: 180).

in their own country living alongside 106 other nationalities, the most prominent of them being Russians, Ukrainians, Germans, Uzbeks, Tatars and Uighurs. They are, however, at present the largest single ethnic group.

The method of deciding key economic questions in the Soviet Union – that is, what should be produced, when, how much, where, how and to whom it should be distributed – was to be by means of a broad national economic plan. The Central Committee of the Communist Party and the Council of Ministers of the USSR became synonymous with the state, which decided all major economic questions. So, Kazakstan as one of the Soviet Republics, carried out all directives of the central bodies.

The Soviet regime also established the third largest coal-producing centre of the USSR in the Karaganda area of Central Kazakstan; it encouraged oil production at Emba and copper mining at Balkash and Karsakpay. The main influence on the fast economic development during the Stalinist era and after came from immigrants from other Republics (Russia, Ukraine, Belarus, Azerbaijan etc.,) as employees of new enterprises. This also occurred during the Second World War.

In 1954 the Virgin Lands[1] project determined the outcome of Kazakstani development as a main producer of wheat and found an inter-republican specialisation for Kazakstan's agricultural sector.

Within Kazakstan, the territory was divided into 19 regions, *oblasts* (see Map 1.2), which were unequally developed. The reason for this was again inter-republican specialisation. In view of this, it is possible to classify all oblasts into four groups (Koshanov, Isaeva, and Yesentugelov, 1993). This classification will include the principle of specialisation and economic-geographical conditions.

The first group, which includes Atyrau (the former Guriev), Aktubinsk, Mangystau (the former Mangyshlak), Western Kazakstan (Uralsk), partially Kzyl-Orda and Jambyl oblasts, is characterised as a group with unique reserves of strategic mineral resources (especially hydrocarbon), and good scientific industrial development potential. Regional priorities defined higher investment activity in Western Kazakstan, where oilfields are located. In the investment structure the Atyrau oblast's share of investment increased from 3.5 per cent in 1981–85 to 7.5 per cent in 1986–90, Western oblast's share increased from 3.8 per cent to 5.1 per cent. The main feature of this group is the non-rational structure[2] of the economy, exceptionally economic and social non-development of the *aul* (village in Central Asia) and also serious ecological problems. In some parts this even extended to destruction of the environment.

The oblasts of *the second group* – Northern Kazakstan, Eastern Kazakstan, Pavlodar, Karaganda, Jezkazgan, Kostanai, and the town Almaty

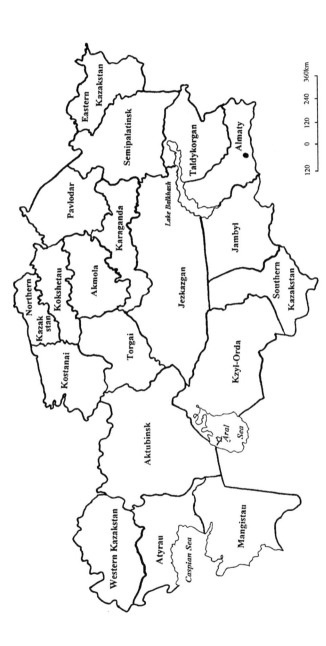

Map 1.2 Regions of Kazakstan
This map is true to the regions in 1996. In 1997 the following changes were announced in the territorial divisions of Kazakstan: Almaty and Taldykorgan were united into a single region – Almaty; were united into a single region – Northern Kazakstan; Semipalatinsk and Eastern Kazakstan; Kokshetau and Northern Kazakstan were united into a single region – Eastern Kazakstan; and Torgai was divided between the regions of Kostanai and Akmola.

(former Alma-Ata) – are oblasts with manufacturing production specialisation with favourable economic conditions for the creation of high technology production. In 1989, for example, the share of the Karaganda oblast in the gross social product (GSP) was the biggest among the 19 oblasts 9.94 per cent. Other industrially developed oblasts produced significant proportions of the GSP (Figure 1.1). At the same time the share of industry was quite high in the Kaz SSR's total volume of industry of all six industrially developed oblasts and the town of Almaty – 38.07 per cent.

The agricultural sector characterises the *third group* of oblasts. Northern Kazakstan, Akmola (Tselinograd), Kostanai, Jambyl, Almaty, Kokshetau, Taldykorgan (Southern Kazakstan), Western Kazakstan. The main agricultural commodity in the Kaz SSR was grain. So, Kaz SSR was one of the leaders among countries such as Canada and Australia in per capita wheat production: 897 kg in 1985 and 967 kg in 1990. Nevertheless, there were some serious distortions which took place in agriculture. The production was the same as in industry: the level of industrial processing of agricultural commodities was very low. The annual per capita production of foodstuffs such as butter, oil, sausages, sugar, fruit and vegetable cannery and food fish production was lower than the average within the USSR. In 1987 the Kaz SSR's processing commodity output accounted for 4.3 per cent of the USSR's volume, while foodstuff accounted for 3.9 per cent. At the same time the population of Kaz SSR was 5.77 per cent of the total population of the USSR.

The oblasts of *the fourth group* – Torgai, Kzyl-Orda, Semipalatinsk, agricultural regions of Atyrau, Mangystau, Jezkazgan and Southern Kazakstan might be called backward regions. Some of them had a lack of attention and investment from the Union government, as the regions were treated as agricultural 'feeder' regions (that is, not producing the final product), and had a generally low level of economic and social investment and development.

As a result of this non-complex development, many oblasts, towns and districts of the Kaz SSR had a standard of living 50–60 per cent of the average level of the Republic as a whole. The analysis of the economic-social development in 1990 had highlighted the most undeveloped towns. These were Temir (Aktyubinsk oblast), Zaisan (Vostochno-Kazakstan oblast), Fort-Shevchenko (Mangistau oblast), Aralsk and Kazalinsk (Kzyl-Orda), Ayaguz and Charsk (Semipalatinsk oblast), Arus (Southern oblast). Therefore in the Kaz SSR, regions were quite different from each other. This manifested itself in the different aspects of social and economic life, for example, industrial development, employment, and welfare.

Obviously every region had its own place in the social system of labour specialisation. As stated earlier, the share of every region in GSP was different and varied from 1.5 per cent (Mangistau oblast) to 9.9 per cent (Karaganda oblast). The share of oblasts in the national income (NI) of the Kaz SSR was changed from 1.8 per cent to 9.5 per cent. There were some territorial differences in the average per capita income. This indicator varied from 58.9 per cent to 119.8 per cent, and is summarised in Table 1.2, in which a significant difference between the regions is clearly expressed.

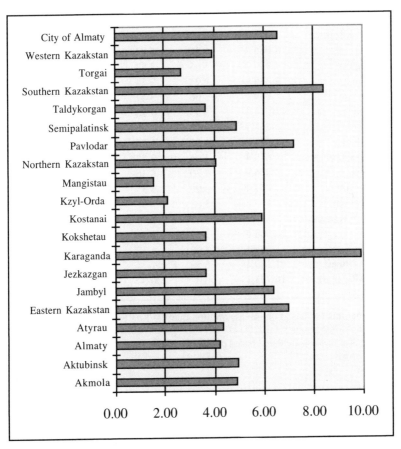

Figure 1.1   Gross social product in Kaz SSR's oblasts, 1990 (*Source*: Table 1.2.)

Table 1.2   Summary of some statistics by oblasts

	Population, 1990 (thousands)	Gross social product (GSP) 1989 (%)	National income (NI) 1989 (%)	Average per capita income, 1990 (%)[a]	Average per capita income, 1990 (roubles)
Akmola	885.4	4.90	4.30	116.78	2 260
Aktubinsk	752.9	4.96	5.56	86.69	1 959
Almaty	993.3	4.17	4.21	74.94	1 450
Atyrau	447.1	4.37	5.14	103.46	2 027
Eastern Kazakstan	949.0	7.02	6.45	104.71	2 122
Jambyl	1 056.4	6.36	6.82	76.90	1 632
Jezkazgan	496.2	3.63	3.87	114.19	1 864
Karaganda	1 339.9	9.94	9.54	119.77	2 232
Kokshetau	669.4	3.66	3.47	102.23	2 282
Kostanai	1 074.4	5.93	4.20	97.34	2 221
Kzyl-Orda	664.9	2.12	2.35	58.86	1 307
Mangistau	331.7	1.52	1.76	159.05	2 079
Northern Kazakstan	610.4	4.05	3.53	102.90	2 139
Pavlodar	956.9	7.20	6.36	102.66	2 196
Semipalatinsk	841.9	4.90	4.55	80.31	1 764
Taldykorgan	731.0	3.63	3.57	93.93	1 657
Southern Kazakstan	1 879.2	8.45	8.94	83.54	1 384
Torgai	304.6	2.67	3.31	157.33	2 177
Western Kazakstan	648.1	3.93	4.32	88.93	1 936
City of Almaty	1 160.4	6.58	7.74	130.13	2 520
Kaz SSR (total)	16 793.1	100.0	100.0	100.0	1 935

[a] Calculations are based on the assumption that the Kaz SSR's average per capita income of 1935 roubles = 100%.
Source: Table was calculated based on data from the State Statistical Committee of the Kaz SSR.

THE KAZAK SOVIET SOCIALIST REPUBLIC IN THE USSR's ECONOMIC SYSTEM

The former Soviet Union constituted a huge integrated system of labour allocation. This meant that the infrastructure of production was spread out across the territory of the former Soviet Union (FSU), with each of the former republics representing a link in the chain. Generally speaking, the division of labour within the USSR republics was not connected to comparative advantage, but rather to a centrally devised plan. All the republic economies (economic regions) were part of the general system *Edinui Narodno Khozhyaistvennyi Komplex* (Integral Economic Complex), which was a system of collective production. Therefore the economic regions represented the interests of the USSR's economic system as a whole. The *Territorial Concept of Labour Division* was very active in Soviet economic science. According to this concept every region (Republic) had to have a particular area of specialisation. Kazakstan possesses vast oil, coal, rare metals, and agricultural resources. In 1988 Kazakstan provided 4.3 per cent of total Soviet Net Material Product (NMP), including 2.5 per cent of total industrial NMP and 6.1 per cent of total agricultural NMP. In this inter-republican specialisation Kazakstan had only two relatively developed fields: the agricultural sector (particularly grain production) and the mining industry (but without production of final products).

Those parts of the manufacturing industry in the Kaz SSR which produced final products did not receive development. According to estimates from the USSR the share of this industrial sector was on average 10 per cent lower than the same average USSR's indicator.

For example, the Kaz SSR's share in the USSR's production of metal-cutting lathes, centrifugal pumps and excavators was only 2 per cent. The share of metal press machines was 3 per cent, fodder harvester combine's share was 4 per cent.

The structure of industrial production is the most important factor in determining the depth and speed of its deterioration. Administratively fixed prices combined with the forced speed of economic growth enforced such disproportion, and led to a deepening difference in supply and

Table 1.3 Kaz SSR percentage share of USSR production

Commodity	Share (%)	Commodity	Share (%)
Electricity	5	Cement	6
Iron ore	10	Phosphorus	90
Coal	18	State grain purchases	18
Chrome ore	95	Wool	24
Lead	70	Meat	7

Source: Kazakstan Research Institute of Economics and Market Relations, Almaty.

demand. This gave way to an overall deficit of resources and hidden inflation. (Kalyuzhnova and Yanovskiy, 1996/97: 3).

During the Soviet period the economic structure was intentionally reshaped in order to make the Kaz SSR an integral part of the Soviet state.

The deformation of the economy caused difficulties in the structure of export-import. Export to foreign countries (excluding other Soviet Republics) was 12 per cent of all production in Kazakstan in 1990. The main components of export were: mineral resources, wool, and silk. The Kazakstani economy was not able to provide the Republic with finished products, therefore this deficit of manufacturing industries led to the dependence of the Kaz SSR upon imports of consumer goods and capital goods. In the total volume of import the share of these products was around 61 per cent in 1990. The export of finished production amounted to only 17 per cent. There is an important industrial sector based on raw materials but the degrees of processing and value added are rather low. In 1990 total Kazakstan trade amounted to 23.5 per cent of the GDP, of which 88.5 per cent was inter-republican trade. For the USSR's economy the main feature was a high degree of economic integration and more or less inter-republican links, which were defined by republican specialisation in the USSR's labour division. For instance, the share of inter-republican turnover in the GSP in Russia was 25 per cent, in the Ukraine it was 34 per cent, and in Kazakstan it was 32 per cent. In the other republics this indicator varied from 46 per cent to 62 per cent.

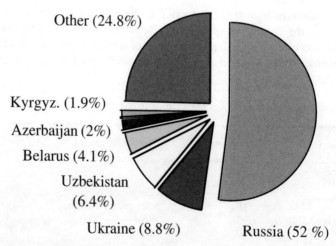

Figure 1.2   Ranking of main trade partners by Kaz SSR in 1987 *(Source*: R. Daviddi and E. Espa, 1995)

In 1990 almost 90 per cent of Kazakstan's trade was within the region of the FSU. The degree of openness of the Kaz SSR towards the other FSU republics has been ranked earlier (Daviddi Yard Espa, 1995), (see Figure 1.2). Kazakstan's degree of dependence upon its major trade partner Russia was above 50 per cent. Exports to Russia were 62 per cent of manufacturing production, including the production of thermal energy (93.8 per cent), oil and gas industry (53.4 per cent), ferrous metallurgy (more than 80 per cent), chemical industry (55.4 per cent), 20 per cent of yellow phosphor, 60 per cent of rubber, 53 per cent polypropylene, 57 per cent of polystirol, and 51 per cent of tyres. The share of imports from Russia was more than 50 per cent in 60 branches of industries. Russian exports to the Kaz SSR were as follows: consumer goods 12 per cent, machine-building 36.5 per cent, energy-bearers 16 per cent, and mining and chemical-forestry industries' production 29 per cent. Up to 1992, trade continued to reflect the historical relationships with Russia, Ukraine and some Central Asian republics to the south.

The Kazakstani specialisation was the product of centralised decision-making, which linked to central planning's priorities to produce relatively high levels of inefficiency.

2 The Years of *Perestroika* in the Kazak Soviet Socialist Republic

The introduction of *Perestroika* in the FSU introduced inertia into the hitherto organised scheme. In real terms, the legislative enactment of *Perestroika* was the replacement of a policy designed for the longer term with short term measures.

The Kaz SSR was one part of a single economic mechanism – the Soviet economy. It is very important to clarify from which point of view we will analyse the economic development of Kaz SSR. The main feature for this period was the over centralisation of Kaz SSR economic activity. As a participant of the Union labour division republic was considered one of the many elements of the Soviet economic life, and therefore it is impossible to analyse the Kaz SSR in this period as a separate economic unit, but only as part of the whole system. *Gosplan* (State Planning Committee) of the USSR had its own point of view on the Kaz SSR's development: the State Planning Committee built plants, enterprises of energy, industry, and transport. A preoccupation with the production sphere was central to the USSR's economic policy in the Kaz SSR. But there was a lack of attention upon infrastructure, and social needs were often neglected. The Communist Party of the Kaz SSR asked Moscow about the proportional development of the industrial, cultural and social spheres (Kunayev, 1992), and the following sections will describe the ensuing developments.

EVENTS OF DECEMBER 1986

Kazakstan passively followed the USSR's reforms in the years of *Perestroika*, When Mikhail Gorbachev was made General Secretary, a new era of political liberalisation was gradually introduced. It is possible to call this a period of '*generation conflict*' between 60–70 year olds and 40–50 year olds. In the USSR the replacement of *nomenklatura* was delayed. *Nomenklatura* could not transfer privileges by right of succession, despite the desire to do so. The average age of the USSR's Politburo was between 65 and 70. Certainly Gorbachev understood that the mentality of the old party *nomenklatura* would be the main difficulty confronting these reforms. Corruption, protectionism, friendly association (of people from the same area) in the republics could also hinder the reforms.

Dinmukhamed Kunayev, 73 years old and the first secretary of the Kazak Communist party, was a good friend of Brezhnev's, and an old member of Communist Party of the Soviet Union (CPSU). For many years he was the leader of Kazakhstan, and under his management the republic was the most developed republic in Central Asia. Of course, there were a lot of negative tendencies, such as strict centralism and protectionism, although this was no more significant than in the other republics. Kunayev knew Kazakhstan and its people, and he enjoyed his authority. At the Sixteenth Congress of the Communist Party of the Kaz SSR, Nursultan Nazarbayev, who was the Chairman of the Council of Ministers of the Kaz SSR, and Kamalidenov, who was the second secretary of the Communist party of the Kaz SSR started to criticise the situation in the republic and Kunayev personally; they proposed significant changes. On the one hand, of course, this criticism generated new impulses to economic observation and thinking, but on the other hand it could be seen as part of a major political struggle between the generations in the Communist Party. The young generation tried to demonstrate to Gorbachev that there were like-minded persons in Kazakhstan, and that he could rely on them. The poor relations between Kunayev and Gorbachev lead Kunayev to prepare a memorandum advising of his decision to retire (on a pension) in 1986, and Gorbachev accepted this.

In December 1986, Gorbachev nominated Gennady Kolbin, who worked as the first secretary of Ul'yanovsk oblast communist party (in Russia) as a first secretary of the Communist Party of the Kaz SSR. Many Kazak people (especially students) demonstrated in Alma-Ata as they disagreed with Moscow's decision concerning the nomination of a person who had never even been in the Kaz SSR before. This political step from the CPSU can be explained as a last attempt by the centre to maintain control in Kazakhstan. However, I here omit detailed consideration of the political implications of this appointment, and concentrate on the economic changes during this period. Kolbin as a protégé of the central administration, tried to keep the same direction of reforms in the Kaz SSR as in the USSR as a whole. It is therefore appropriate to consider this period through the Soviet concept of *Perestroika*.

MANAGEMENT, PLANNING AND CONTROL IN THE KAZ SSR

The planning, management and control of enterprises was undertaken within the framework of the Kazakstani command economy and system of state ownership and management in the Kaz SSR and the USSR as a whole. Undoubtedly the most common property form was the bureaucratic state-owned enterprise (for example, see Kornai, 1992), which covered key industries such as mining, energy production, foreign trade and finance, and which enabled the domination of non-state and non-key industrial sectors. The state-owned form constituted the property of the 'whole of the people' and could be defined by: the disposal of their residual income into the central state budget (the definition of what is residual income is itself decide by the state); their not being objects for purchase or sale, lease, gift nor inheritance; and their property rights of control over the activity of the enterprise being exercised by the state bureaucracy, normally directly by the lower levels of the hierarchical bureaucracy.

Another important property form was the co-operative, particularly within the agricultural sector, and often as a legacy of the enforced and mostly brutal collectivisation of the land and population in Kazakstan during the late 1920s and early 1930s. Rather than being voluntary associations, in the Kaz SSR this can be characterised as follows: members were not free to refuse to join or to leave the co-operative, or to employ outside labour or be employed as outside labour; the leadership was only formally elected by the membership, and was often an appointed member of the Union bureaucracy (often through the republican authorities), who in turn was dependent on upper levels of the bureaucracy; the leadership had no authority to make independent decisions about using the co-operatives income, alienation of the co-operative's means of production and how the means of production would be used. In fact these decisions were taken at the upper levels of the bureaucracy, and co-operativisation provided little distinction to direct state ownership (Kornai, 1992).

The state system of governance of enterprises within the Union and Kaz SSR was at two levels: functional committees, at both Union and republican levels, having no direct supervision of enterprises, but which were responsible for overall policy and planning (*GosPlan* of USSR and *GosPlan* of Kaz SSR) and certain subordinate aspects of economic life such as supply (*GosSnab* of USSR and GosSnab of Kaz SSR), labour (*GosTrud* of USSR and *GosTrud* of Kaz SSR); and, branch ministries to which enterprises were in direct subordination, and which were responsible for translating directives of the functional committees into concrete operating decisions for the enterprises. Branch ministries were of three types: *soyuznye* (all-Union, controlling enterprises directly from Moscow); *soyuzno-respublicanskie* (Union-republican, which were linked to affiliated ministries within Kaz SSR where there was a need for more management decentralisation in industries such as food-processing with numerous smaller enterprises); and, *respublicanskie* (republican, having their headquarters in Kaz SSR, and directly supervising sectors which were focused on local needs such as intra-republic transportation, and which were subordinate to the Union-republican ministries).

The supervisory functions of the ministries comprised: strategic planning of enterprises following directive from functional committees, and involving such areas as mergers of divisions, developing and financing of new facilities and diversification of products; research and development; and operational planning including annual production targets, product mix and wages; and staffing. The latter included the appointment of senior enterprise managers by direction of the supervising ministry. This ensured enterprise managers in Kaz SSR were dependent and obligated to the functional committee bureaucrats in Moscow. In turn, the most successful enterprise managers were recruited to the branch ministries (Kossov and Gurkov, 1995).

The Central Committee of the Communist Party of the Kaz SSR was dominant over the state governance system, and contained within it departments of industry, agriculture, for example, which supervised the activities of all economic activity of the Republic. At the micro-level every enterprise had two controllers who often had conflicting interests: the branch ministry and the local committee of the Communist Party (*Raicom*). The minister's goal was for each enterprise to achieve targets based on Union and republican directives. The objectives for the Communist Party were similar, but in addition viewed the resources of local enterprises as a social resource (and 'Party resource') which could be utilised by the Party. This meant that enterprise managers could be forced to send their workers to harvest, construct houses, and to invest in local needs such as road maintenance. This led to additional waste of resources and production (the primary aim of enterprises), when one day workers would be in the factory, the next day, for example, would be in the fields or assisting the police with enforcement of public highway regulations. However, despite trying to satisfy these dual and often contradictory objectives, enterprise managers could be called to account for targets not met by their Party controllers.

We can look at the co-ordination mechanisms (which involve both vertical and hierarchical linkages), operating on and within enterprises in Kaz SSR. *Bureaucratic co-ordination* describes the vertical linkages which existed within the control mechanisms imposed on enterprises in Kaz

SSR, although this did not conform to the classic model of hierarchy as we have seen in the overlap between state and party apparatus. In both state-owned and co-operative enterprises, management was dependent on functional ministries, and subordinate to the (political) needs of the republican and Union bureaucracy.

Self-governing co-ordination was underdeveloped in Kaz SSR until the late 1980s (which we describe later in this chapter). The nominal character of co-operative enterprises were of self-governance, but only vestiges of a system of proposals or criticisms from below pertained in practice.

Ethical co-ordination would apply to the motivation of those in enterprises who were prepared to give up their personal time, and make sacrifices for the good of the enterprise. This occurred in the 1930s and 1940s. After this ethical and bureaucratic co-ordination became intertwined in that the giving up of personal time (for example, *Kommunisticheskii Subbotnik* – Communist Saturday) was mostly subject to compulsion rather than based on altruism, a feeling of community and/or political conviction.

Despite the erosion of the traditional family in Kazakstan, there is evidence that family traditions and ties have survived despite sovietisation and collectivisation. In part, marriage amongst ethnic Kazaks was based on strict exogamy, which required detailed knowledge of family relationships (Akiner, 1995; Olcott, 1995), although this only applied to *aul* (indigenous Kazak village) community. *Family co-ordination mechanisms* operated in the town conditions, within and between enterprises, for ethnic Kazak people. For example, those coming from *aul* to the town who had gained a position would endeavour to provide opportunities for relatives coming to the town in order to obtain employment.

The motivation for top managers of enterprises in Kaz SSR to perform may have been varied: political and moral conviction towards party ideas and the enterprise plan's objectives; identification with the job and the self-satisfaction from a job well done; power; prestige; material benefits; a quiet life free from problems with superiors and subordinates; and fear of punishment. Because the managers were not owners of these enterprises, and were essentially employees rather than entrepreneurs, they were not likely to be highly motivated by the need to achieve. It was likely that these motivators acted on the management of enterprises in varying forms, and to a large extent flowed from the degree to which conviction to party ideas could be demonstrated, and the strategic and operating objectives handed down from the state bureaucracy.

In Kaz SSR there were two types of state enterprise: those administered by the Kaz SSR and those directly run by the central USSR authorities.

The latter were directly controlled by the Moscow bureaucracy and received more economic benefits (investment, material and other resources) and consequently more attention and prestige. These enterprises produced materials and goods of prime importance to the Union, and received their directions straight from Moscow. Managers within these enterprises therefore tended to be more competent and efficient, as the best tended to be recruited to these enterprises.

We can therefore see the strong dependencies on the Union bureaucracy which enterprise management developed. Not only was this a vertical dependency, but also a psychological one, where enterprise managers were unable to make independent decisions. It was within this context that, at the end of the 1980s with the introduction of *Perestroika* within the USSR and then gradually in Kaz SSR, the ground began to shift so that enterprises in Kaz SSR had now to look more towards their own economic programmes and dependencies, rather than towards those handed down through the machinery of the Union bureaucracy.

'INTENSIFICATION 90' PROGRAMME

The five year plan for 1986–90 was defined by the slogan *uskorenie*, or acceleration of economic growth. The main basis for this was a programme of increasing investment in machine-building which ultimately led to deadlock of the economy.

In 1985 the proportion that Kaz SSR's machine-building produced of the total USSR volume was 1.8 per cent, at the same time this indicator for Russia was 65.8 per cent; Ukraine, 18.8 per cent; and Belarus, 4.2 per cent. The Kazak machine-building industry constituted undeveloped plants which produced final products: instruments, radio engineering, motor cars, etc. The Kaz SSR's needs in machine-building were supplied from other republics (see Table 2.1), and the technical level of machines, equipment, apparatus, and instruments produced in Kaz SSR was behind both that of the rest of the USSR and foreign machinery.

Generally speaking, machine-building in the Kaz SSR was dominated by repair plants. Ninety per cent of all machine-building plants were repair plants. This can be attributed to the fact that a lot of the equipment was in poor repair and depreciated, and needed constant maintenance. For example, repair work on a tractor during its lifetime was 3–6 times higher than the tractor's value, and the labour inputs of repair were higher than the labour inputs for producing a new tractor by a factor of 6–10. Changes in this situation were impossible for the Kaz SSR, because the labour

Table 2.1   Dependence of Kaz SSR's industries in USSR's machine-building production

Industry	Export of machine-building production from other republics (%)
Electroenergy	100
Oil extraction	90–95
Oil-processing and gas	100
Coal	70–75
Ferrous metallurgy	90–93
Non-ferrous metallurgy	80–85
Chemical and oil-chemical	85–90
Machine-building and metal-cutting	90–95
Wood and woodworking	100
Building materials	100
Cotton	100
Food	100
Agriculture	65–70
Stock-raising	70–75

Source: Based on material from the Research Institute of Economics and Market Relations, Almaty, Kazakstan.

division for the Kaz SSR was never supposed to create an effective machine-building complex. In 1990 machine-building was only 16.3 per cent of the total volume of the Kaz SSR's industrial production, compared to the overall USSR indicator of 30 per cent. According to the programme of 'Intensification 90' a lot of investment must be transferred from other branches of industry to the machine-building complex. A lack of active governmental policy, which was supposed to lead to development of technical progress, and unsatisfactory economic reform did not allow machine-building in Kaz SSR to achieve significant results. Table 2.2 shows the main results in machine-building during the last (XII) five-year plan, and as we can see the actual 'putting into operation' of basic funds declined by a quarter. This means that investment, which was redistributed to machine-building from the other branches of industry, was not effective. In 1990 this act raised the problem of structural distortions in the Kazak economy. The investment cycle was very long, and this defined the failure of 'Intensification 90', as the *dolgostroi* ('delayed construction') became worse and worse, becoming the defining step in the decline of machine-building production.

Table 2.2   The main indicators of machine-building development

Indicator	1981–85	1986–90
Putting into operation of basic production assets (% from total volume on the end of the period)	42.1	33.0
Leaving from operation of basic production assets (% from total volume on the end of the period)	17.4	24.4

Source: Goskomstat Kaz SSR (1991), *Statisticheskii ezhegodnik Kazakstana* (Annual statistics of Kazakstan) Alma-Ata.

In terms of production factors it is possible to observe rapid rising costs instead of growth of output. Why did this happen? The main explanation for this is the intrinsic cost-inducing (*zatratnii*) character of the Soviet economy.[1] The Soviet economic mechanism orientated industries and enterprises to increase costs. In another words: the structure predetermines excessive costs. Large investment has been wasted, and the prioritising of development of machine-building in investment did not materialise.

THE LAW ON ENTERPRISE AND *KHOZRASCHYOT*

The general principles of *Perestroika* were introduced through economic laws such as the Law on Co-operatives and the Law on Individual Labour Activity. These laws constituted the first steps towards private entrepreneurship and the development of the private sector.

In 1987 a new USSR law on enterprise was introduced. From one perspective this law was the start of the collapse of the Soviet economic system. The main principle of this law was that all state enterprises were to become self-financing (*khozraschot*) and more responsible for their own results of production. Therefore the law was considered to expand the freedom of state enterprises. One of the main ways in which this law was implemented was a new price policy on the microlevel. This meant that enterprises had an opportunity to discriminate prices of a good. 'Officially, compulsory plan targets were abolished; in reality, they remained in watered-down form'. (Aslund, 1995: 29). It was a year when the notion of 'republican *khozraschyot*' became part of the economic life of the republics. According to this notion, republics had to be given more independent powers, including the authority to manage their own finances. In many respects, enterprise law and *khozraschyot* contradicted each other. While enterprises received more freedom in economic decisions, they still remained dependent on the state. However, *khozraschyot* could only function if enterprises were independent; that is, had property rights. In this case workers as owners would be able to participate in management. In Soviet society ownership belonged to people, and nobody felt responsibilities for *narodnuyu* (publicly owned) property (the property of these people). So the basic premise of this law on enterprise failed to satisfactorily account for the logical consequences of the state enterprise's reaction to this scheme. Given the freedom to decide on the distribution of their production funds (the income of enterprises), they focused strongly on the wage base. In addition they tended to alter their production focus towards more expensive goods, which resulted in increasing incomes of enterprises,[2] hidden inflation and a shortage of consumer goods.

The new forms of economic life in the Kaz SSR such as *khozraschyot* and self-financing were reached without any economic basis and without establishing realistic long-term measures for materialising this. *Arenda* (lease) relations in agricultural terms were used in all agricultural units.

Meanwhile the progress of economic indicators during 1986–90 was very moderate. Annual growth of inputs took place for production of one unit of production for example, the real cost of one head of grain increased by 25.9 per cent, potato respectively by 21 per cent, meat by 26.3 per cent, and so on. Growth of goodwill and compensation for losses were reached because of the increase in the purchasing prices.

Khozraschyot in consumer service was carried out formally in the Kaz SSR. The income of enterprises did not cover expenditures. The same situation also took place in transport.

The negative side of expanding independence in an enterprise's use of funds was the distribution of these funds to solve a short-term problem – rise of wages. The introduction of the latest machinery and technology was neglected. In other words, enterprises were given visible rights but few responsibilities, and this practice led to monetary imbalance. Generally during the XII five-year plan the income of the population in Kaz SSR was 129 billion roubles; at the same time, realisation of this income was only 124 billion roubles. In 1990 the money supply increased by 2.5 times and reached 5.8 per cent of the income of the population compared to 3.8 per cent in 1985. The highest level of this was in Kzyl-Orda, Kokshetau, Aktubinsk, Jeskazgan, Taldykorgan and Uralsk oblasts. The increase of income, which was not supported by goods and services, exacerbated an inflationary overhang.

The situation was exacerbated by the introduction of the Republican *Khozraschyot*. The main principles of the enterprise *khozraschyot* were transferred to the republican level, which exaggerated their effects. According to the inter-republican labour division some of the republics had developed manufacturing production (such as Belarus, Russia, Latvia, Estonia, etc.); some of them had mining industry, mineral and agricultural sources as the main area of labour specialisation (Kazakstan, Uzbekistan, and others). Increasingly and damagingly, there evolved a demarcation between *kormiliszu* (republics who provide) and *potrebiteli* (republics who consume). To some extent this demarcation was based on erroneous assumptions. For example, some researchers consider 'Kazakstan and Central Asian republics were primary recipients of large net transfers of funds from the Soviet central budget amounting in some cases to about ten per cent of their GDP'. (Orlowski 1995: 5). However, the reality is a different explanation of such subsidies from Moscow. It is necessary to remark that only raw materials were exported to the world market, when at the same time the finished products which were produced in the USSR were of low quality and their domestic prices were inappropriately high. In an average year Kazakstan would receive a subsidy of 4–6 billion roubles, whilst at the same time the disparity of prices meant Kazakstan lost 7–9 billion roubles (data from Kazakstan Research Institute of Economics and Market Relations). Thus the idea of regional *khozraschyot* within a unitary state such as USSR was political, and became the main economic reason of the collapse of the central planned system.

The programme of 'Intensification 90' comprised some smaller scale programmes aimed at solving specific social problems. The next element of the economic policy of the time was the programme 'Housing (*Zhil'e*) 91'.

THE PROGRAMME 'HOUSING (*ZHIL'E*) 91'

The programme of housing, '*Zhil'e* 91', was established by the Kazak government in 1985. According to this programme every family would be provided an individual apartment or house by 1991. Of course this programme was unrealistic, but nevertheless '*Zhil'e* 91' had substantial success in 1988, when builders commissioned 8.9 million square metres of housing. Growth rate of investment in house-construction was considered a priority, constituting 32 per cent of the total investment volume in the Kazak economy in 1986–90. The share of investment in house-construction increased from 16.8 per cent to 21.9 per cent. This shift in investment structure can be explained as a result of the implementation of the programme 'Housing 91'. During 1986–90 11.5 billion roubles were invested in house-construction, but the housing problem was far from solved (Table 2.3).

Table 2.3 Commissioning of dwelling houses (thousand square metres of total living space)

1985	1986	1987	1988	1989	1990
6 627	6 758	8 303	8 779	8 618	7 820

Source: Goskomstat Kaz SSR (1991), *Statisticheskii ezhegodnik Kazakstana* (Annual statistics of Kazakstan) Alma-Ata.

Nevertheless, between 1987–90 602.3 thousand families had improved their housing conditions. Among that number 502.3 thousand families had been in the queue, according to the programme of housing ('Zhil'e 91'). One of the positive consequences of this programme for Kazakstan was the decrease in the housing queue, which was a significant issue for the population. The programme decreased the time queuing for flats by 70 per cent, by means of individual house-building, co-operative building, and young building co-operatives (*MZhK-molodezhnui zhilishnui kooperativ*). However, about 40 per cent of the housing fund of the republic were not of the required quality, and 4.1 million square metres of housing were classified as dilapidated. No attempts were made to address the specific needs for job creation.

FOOD PROGRAMME

According to this programme in Kazakstan subsidiary small-holdings and farms attached to factories were developed to an extent. The mechanism of implementation was as follows: an industrial enterprise included in its organisational structure a collective farm or state farm, or the enterprise rented land, bought dairy cattle, etc., with the aim of improving the supply of foodstuffs for their workers.

For the period 1985–90, the average per head consumption of meat increased from 72 kg in 1985 to 92 kg in 1990 and of milk from 301 kg to 337 kg. (Goskomstat Republic of Kazakstan, 1995: 231).

The main disadvantage of this programme was that enterprises and organisations were forced into unusual functions, ones in which they had not previously dealt. The value of final agricultural production was high, and was loaded onto the costs of enterprises. One of the economic explanations of this phenomenon was again the disparity of prices between agriculture and industry. Prices were created using political as opposed to economic criteria, with labour costs consistently artificially low. The purpose of the programme was to eliminate the population's unsatisfied demand for food. In some respects this problem was solved. Nevertheless, because of the specialisation of these enterprises, the quality and efficiency of production was markedly low. These measures could not fulfil the needs of the market and decrease inflationary pressure. Of course this production was non-competitive, and thus could not be in high demand even upon the domestic market. On the creation of this line of production, high expenditure decreased the economic situation.

II

The New National Economy:
the Learning Curve

II

3 The Beginning of Sovereignty and the End of the Rouble Zone

The political leadership crisis in the spring of 1991 exerted a negative influence upon the process of economic transformation in the USSR. The government of the USSR did not properly manage any of the programmes of reform. The coup attempt in August collapsed the fundamental structure of the Soviet Union and resulted in its dissolution. Having considered the historical conditions from which new countries emerged, we now turn our attention to the collapse of the Soviet Union, which created new 'Independent' States. The Kazakstani Parliament had announced the independence of Kazakstan on 16 December 1991, and Nursultan Nazarbayev was elected the President of Kazakstan.

The legacy which Kazakstan inherited from the economic system of the Soviet Union resulted in the republic having only two relatively developed fields of economic structure: the agricultural sector (particularly grain production) and the mining industry (but without the production of final products). The policy approach in the republics of the former Soviet Union has been to emphasise price liberalisation and the elimination of subsidies, fiscal stabilisation, monetary restraint and trade liberalisation with less consideration given to reforms of a structural nature. Predominant in policy debates has been the emphasis given to establishing independent currencies, and the negotiation of bilateral economic arrangements with Russia in the post reform era.

THE GEOPOLITICAL SITUATION

Kazakstan will always feel a dependence on geographical neighbours, and it needs to build a national strategy which takes its neighbour countries' interests into consideration. To an extent, the Kazakstani concept of sovereignty was immature in 1991. Whereas relationships with neighbouring countries prior to 1991 were the responsibility of central government, after 1991 the new Kazakstani government had to learn quickly to take the position of its neighbours and allies into account when formulating policy.

Between 1991 and 1993 Kazakstani experienced a sort of geopolitical 'honeymoon', in the sense that the concept of *independent* was not initially understood. The legacy of central government extended into foreign relations, and despite rhetoric, the initial steps into international relations were tentative. Numerous well-publicised meetings with world leaders gave the misleading impression that Kazakstan was well advanced in the process of assimilation into and acceptance upon the world stage.

However, economic factors were not necessarily connected with these initial geopolitical moves, but as economic development progressed it became apparent that foreign relations and economic development would inevitably be interdependent. It is clear that there is an intimate, symbiotic relationship between the somewhat tortured and definitely problematic process of economic transition, and geopolitical relationship development. (Kalyuzhnova, and Tucker, 1997: 18)

Kazakstan perceived national interests in terms of political and economic interests. However, parallel to the question of geopolitical maturity was the question of economic security. This arose in the very early years of Kazakstani independence. The formation and survival of the Newly Independent States (NIS) depends in large measure on economic factors, and it is essential to achieve a degree of satisfaction of demand for goods and services within the country, which would provide protection from that degree of external influence which might be considered dangerous for the normal economic functioning of a country. Multifunctional economic security might be characterised as economic security controlling the stability of economic national interests as well as restraint on the national interests of a country in political and economic matters. Machowski (Machowski, 1985: 5–18) suggests the following criteria regarding related economic security:

1. Reduction to the minimum of dependence upon partners for important economic parameters (expanding of political freedom);
2. The normal degree of economic dependence must be defined for every case, especially with consideration for partner's medium term interests.

Regarding economic security, it is necessary to consider the degree of vulnerability and the threat to the realisation of opportunity. Vulnerability is understood in this sense as the degree of dependence upon partners. When the variant is worst (changes in external links), the dependence is sharpest. This would provoke new costs due to adaptation to the new situation, and in some respects may cause insurmountable problems for the

Kazakstani economy. In reality, dependence is a necessary condition in the loss of economic security. This process of imbalance arose with the creation of dependency and restriction of access to labour, material, technical and other resources.

The creation of a stable system of economic security is especially important in the current period for Kazakstan, as the young state takes its initial steps along the road towards independence. The question is which economic sectors to prioritise. The set of sectors which were absolutely essential to prioritise in order to encourage economic security in the republic are:[1]

1. Sectors which provide the republic with food. The annual growth in agricultural production and essential goods and services must not be less than the specific increase in population.
2. Sectors which provide for the normal functioning of the economy as a whole (transport, communications, equipment production, construction materials). Changes in growth must provide for the minimal needs of the economy in the case of the breakdown of external economic links.
3. Sectors which are connected with the development of raw materials. At present this is the only sector bringing hard currency to the republic budget, which allows the modernisation of the production apparatus and the technical and technological base.

INITIAL ATTEMPTS AT REFORM

The process of transforming a planned economy is complex, and even under the best of circumstances it entails large difficulties and transition costs. Debates have been conducted on the relative merits of macroeconomic stabilisation and economic liberalisation; on the gradual versus the shock-therapy approach to policy reform and on the required level of institutional development.

After 1991 Kazakstan had the opportunity to conduct its own national economic policy, which allowed the new state to enter in the world market. In a country with a post-planned economy the package of reforms were the same at the beginning of transition: privatisation, taxation, regulation of inflation, interest rate, unemployment, investment policy, changes of economic structure, etc. The principal difference and explanation of the different results of this policy is the approach and quality of the implementation of economic strategy in practice and the initial conditions (Box 3.1).

The New National Economy

By 1991, after the *Perestroika* period, Kazakstan had inherited a deteriorating economy with falling output, rising prices and increasing shortages. Therefore, the new Kazakstani government had the difficult task of amending macroeconomic stability to provide initial conditions for improving living standards, and for encouraging economic growth.

In this period a great deal of debate took place regarding the correct approach for the economic independence of Kazakstan. For example, one of the most popular ideas, encouraged by the World Bank, was the Kazakstan had to expand exports outside the CIS (World Bank, 17 March 1992). Generally this was a good idea, but due to the circumstances (strong inter-republican links, the non-competitiveness of Kazakstani production, a lack of final production, etc.) this project was unrealistic at that time. One of the negative consequences of this idea was the break-up of inter-republican economic relations, which led to a greater decline in economic activity. External factors, such as the difficult process of the establishment of the other newly independent states, the position of Russia, and so on, complicated the overall situation. In this period Kazakstan became a field of intellectual exercises by international organisations who all recommended different economic programmes. In some cases these programmes contradicted each other, in other cases a lack of knowledge of local situation led to serious mistakes. Foreign investors and commentators in the developed world were very enthusiastic about the future of Kazakstan, and predicted a large inflow of foreign investments and an economic future along the lines of the Asian 'tigers' (South Korea, Taiwan, for example) for the young country.

> In a lot of countries the strategy of accelerated development of quick economic growth was successfully adopted, including West Germany (in the immediate post-war period), South Korea, Singapore, Taiwan, Hong Kong (in later decades). The situation of these countries at the beginning, excluding direct entrance to sea and ocean ways,was worse than that of Kazakstan today. From this point as well as taking into consideration the increasing of mega-tendencies in the sphere of science, new technologies and management, integration and world economic links, it is possible to compress the time of transition of Kazakstan to new condition to 15–20 years. (Nazarbayev, 1992a: 9).[2]

President Nazarbayev had strong 'South Korean' preferences, and in 1991 appointed Dr Chan Yang Bang (who was previously a professor in San Francisco), foreign economic adviser to the president. All intellectual resources were concentrated on the creation of an effective economic programme. The common conclusion, reached through analysis of the current economic situation, was that during the Soviet period Kazakstan had economic dependence upon the other Soviet republics, and the time had come to establish a new economic policy, directed at foreign investors, to develop oil and gas resources, to enter into the world market and so on. Whilst the outlook was promising at face value, on closer analysis it appears to consist more of slogans than of actual economic implementation. This lack of systematic measures took place in the initial stage of transition. The World Bank, the International Monetary Fund (IMF) and other international organisations sent missions and advisory groups which tried to help. The main argument was that local economists and experts were unable to evaluate the strategy towards market reforms because of the legacy of the previous period, and 'old' knowledge could not be adapted to the creation of a modern view. It would be a mistake to say that all of the recommendations were not applicable for Kazakstan. The implementation of these recommendations had difficulties at different levels, and sometimes the government tried to link different approaches, expecting positive results. The obvious question, about the creation of one coherent programme of economic transformation, was raised by the end of 1992.

Box 3.1   Kazakstan in the last years of USSR economic review

The economic structure of Kazakstan was not changed in the last years of the 1980s. The percentage of changing population and production compared with the USSR practically did not change (Table 3.1). In these years a moderate but constant growth of production took place in Kazakstan. This growth was higher than in Russia, but less than in the other republics of the Central Asia.

Table 3.1   Kazakstan in the USSR, 1980s (% from union indicator)

Indicator	1980	1985	1990
Population	5.6	5.7	5.8
Produced national income	4.6	4.8	5.8
Construction	6.0	5.9	5.7
Distributed banking credit	5.6	6.0	6.9
Average monthly wage of workers and employees (USSR = 1.00)	0.99	0.98	0.97

Source: Table was composed based on data from Source A.

Box 3.1 Continued

The character of changing GNP in Kazakstan corresponded to the USSR's level. The income and material benefits which the population received were the same as in the other republics of the USSR, but a bit less than in Russia. Considering that the growth of population was 1.2 per cent in this period, the income per head did not increase.

Table 3.2 Kazakstan and other republics of the USSR

	Kazakstan	Russia	USSR	Republics of Central Asia and Kazakstan
Growth of population, 1979–89 (%)	1.2	0.7	0.9	2.4
Infant mortality rate (per 1000 live births), 1989	25.9	17.8	22.7	38.7
Area (thousands of sq. km)	2 717	17 075	22 402	3 994
Population (millions) 1989	16.5	147.4	289	49.3

Source: A.

Infant mortality rate (per 1000 live births) was 26, lower than in Europe (30), but higher than the average infant mortality rate in USSR (Table 3.2). Life expectancy was 69 years. The indicator of the literacy of population was the same as the indicator in developed countries.

The system of monetary control erased inflation, which led to the union budget deficit, and automatically transferred all these problems to the republics. In 1991 GNP in Kazakstan decreased by 7 per cent. The main explanation of this is the crisis in the production sphere. Drought was the reason of the decline in agricultural production. This indicator is estimated to have declined by 16 per cent. In the financial area Kazakstan experienced difficulties which were the consequence of the central planning system, where social funds were distributed and re-distributed, and there was a lack of attention regarding macroeconomic stability. As a rule, the largest part of budget revenue was collected from state-owned enterprises, via income tax or turnover tax. Distribution via subsidies was the main feature of this system, and Kazakstan received its own share from the Central Budget. The contribution to Kazakstan from the Union budget was 10 per cent of GDP in 1989 and declined in 1991 by 6.7 per cent (Table 3.3).

Table 3.3   State financial operations (% from GNP)

	1988	1989	1990	1991
Revenue	25.8	26.7	22.8	21.1
Expenditures	34.6	36.6	33.4	36.0
Transfers from the union budget	8.2	9.8	9.3	6.7
Balance excluding gratuitous funds	−8.8	−10.9	−10.6	−14.7

Source: A.

In 1991 the budget deficit achieved 8 per cent of GNP with transfers from the Central Budget. This was a result of the changing of financial policy – cutting revenue from Union budget, and increasing expenditure.

INDUSTRY AND INVESTMENT

The key to economic revival lies in the industrial sector. The situation in industry became worse in the first years of independence. As we can see, the net material product (NMP) fell by 37 per cent between 1990 and 1992. Industrial output had fallen by 27.2 per cent between 1990 and 1993 (Table 3.4).

Very sharp falls of investment occurred in Kazakstan in 1990–93, when investment demand suffered from economic austerity policies and economic uncertainty (Figure 3.1). The fall in gross fixed investment volume was 69.6 per cent in Kazakstan in 1993 compared with 1989. The efficiency of the investment process also suffered, as is indicated by rising gestation periods.

The total volume of investment between 1990 and 1993 decreased by 68 per cent, including two thirds of all investment in the production sphere. The share of investment in GNP changed from 26 per cent in 1990

Table 3.4   Industrial output (% change in output, 1990 = 100%)

	1990	1991	1992	1993
Industrial output	100	99.1	85.4	72.8

Source: Table was calculated based on data from *Statisticheskii Yezhegodnik Kazakhstana 1991, 1994*.

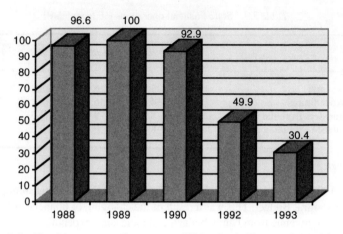

Figure 3.1 Fixed investment (in constant 1991 prices) (*Source*: *Statisticheskii Ezhegodnik Kazakhstana, 1991*: 367, *1994*: 235)

to 23.5 per cent in 1993. Investment as a factor of future development in Kazakstan is becoming a problem. Eighty per cent of government resources were used in construction of enterprises; and 42–46 per cent of investments were used in Vostochno-Kazakstanskaya, Mahgistauskaya, Semipalatinskaya, Torgaiskaya oblasts. In general the volume of building-assembly works in 1992–93 decreased by 65.5 per cent.

In production, construction investments were used particularly in basic branches of the economy: 20.7 per cent state investments – on development of electro-energy, 16.0 per cent – coal industry, 14.0 per cent – oil industry. The reduction of the investment activity had a negative effect on machine-building, chemical industry, oil-chemical industry, and the fuel industry. Investments in fuel industry in 1993 decreased 2.4 times, and in machine-building 2.8 times. In all these industries the quantity of retirement funds as an active part of the basic funds in 1993 amounted to more than was actually put into their operation.

Enterprises were not able to create financial resources to continue production, because under the rise in prices of resources the size of depreciation decreases by a third. According to specialists from the Kazakstan Research Institute of Economics and Market Relations, the rates of deprecation on reimbursement as a whole were regularly reduced (Figure 3.2).

This period was one when the financial resources of enterprises did not play a significant role in the formation of investments. They were financed by centralised sources. The share of depreciation relative to investments in 1975 was 24.6 per cent, in 1980 it was 30.0 per cent, in 1985, 35.8 per cent, and in 1990, 41.2 per cent. This rate was reduced to 5.5 per cent in 1993.

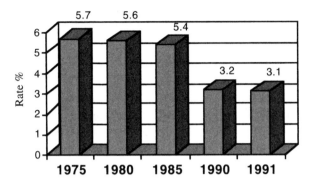

Figure 3.2 The depreciation rate in Kazakstan (%) (*Source*: Data of the Kazakstan Research Institute of Economics and Market Relations)

The reason why the reproduction of basic funds was impossible was that the cost structure of production was being transformed. Inflation was a constraint upon renovation of industrial apparatus, and the degree of wear of basic funds in different branches was 42.2–47.5 per cent. The reason for this was the inefficient work of machine-building. The co-efficient of funds retirement provisions was only 1 per cent in 1993. In 1985 33 per cent of investments from the total volume were put into funds renovation; in 1992 16 per cent. In 1993 only 2.7 per cent of industrial investments were put into machine-building as a main industrial branch for technical progress.

Therefore, in economic terms, the crisis situation in the investment sphere was defined by reasons which are reflected in the financial crisis:

1. a decrease in the volume of centralised financial resources, followed by adequate growth in the use of decentralised resources in inflationary conditions;
2. high taxes and reduction of production, and as a consequence, a decrease in the real volume of investment;
3. a decrease in depreciation charges as a source of investment, an underdeveloped government mechanism for investment regulation, an undeveloped securities market, and a small inflow of foreign capital.

The transition to a market economy after 1990 has led to structural changes. The large falls in industrial output demonstrated that structural changes were absolutely necessary for the newly established states (some industries improving, some others declining rapidly). By 1993 in some transitional countries, signs of economic recovery were observed (Poland, Slovenia, etc.), but in Kazakstan contraction of output continued throughout

1993. Macroeconomic performance in Kazakstan in 1993 turned out to be generally worse than the Kazakstani government expected.

FOREIGN ECONOMIC RELATIONS

As we mentioned in the first chapter, the bulk of Kazakstan's external trade used to take place within the USSR. Until the break-up of the USSR, there were no barriers on trade within the republics of the USSR. After the declaration of independence, Kazakstan concluded trading agreements with other partners of the CIS. Initially, trade within the CIS was conducted in roubles. It came through the settlements accounts of the republican state banks (*Gosbanks*), and the clearance time ranged from two days to two months. At the same time inflation rose, which led to barter terms of trade, or to settlement in foreign currency. This was repeated again and again: it was required to accelerate payment settlements among enterprises engaged in intra-CIS trade.

Russia was still the main trade partner for Kazakstan during the first years of independence. For example, in 1993 the Russian share of export of industrial production in Kazakstan was 72 per cent of the total amount.

Trade outside the CIS was isolated during the Soviet period. Such trade was conducted through Moscow, and composed only 5 per cent of GDP in 1991. The statistical data on Kazakstani foreign trade show this very clearly (Table 3.5), and the export per capita for Kazakstan was only US$ 76.

The government of Kazakstan tried to establish and develop relations with countries outside CIS. The government very much hoped to generate income through trade of oil and gas for modernisation and rehabilitation of industries. To evolve this expansion and diversification of Kazakstani international trade, the government negotiated a number of bilateral agreements with countries such as Austria, Bulgaria, Egypt, Hungary, and the

Table 3.5   Kazakstani foreign trade indicators, 1993 (*in US$ millions*)

1992		1993	
Export	*Import*	*Export*	*Import*
1 398	469	1 318	364

Source: Vneshnyaya torgovlya respubliki Kazakstan so stranami dalnego zarubezh'ya v 1993 godu, 1994: 4.

USA, which awarded Kazakstan most favoured nation (MFN) status in March 1993. (Central Asian Republics, 1996, Volume I: 32).

AGRICULTURE

There are large areas of land available for agriculture in Kazakstan. The general picture of the functioning of the agricultural sector is demonstrated in Table 3.6.

In 1990, 1336 (53 per cent) collective and state farms used land leasing as the prime principle of running agricultural development. Collective and state farms began to operate on a cost-accounting and self-financing basis, which gave them progressive results in the production of agricultural goods. The average annual volume of agricultural production increased by 15.4 per cent in 1986–90, including the state sector (by 14.4 per cent) and the individual sector (by 18.6 per cent). Kazakstan was one of the former USSR republics with an exportable grain surplus.

The total volume of agricultural manufacturing industries increased by 21.3 per cent by 1990. But the level of development of manufacturing industries in agriculture lagged behind the needs of the population. The amount of farm produce, such as dairy products, vegetable oil, cooked meats, sugar, confectionery, canned fruit, vegetables and so on, per person was lower than in the USSR as a whole, and the problem of maximum self-material security remained acute.

The main question raised in that time was that of land reform. The authorities indicated that private ownership of land was not under consideration for the time being. Of course on the populist level they recognised that private ownership plays a crucial role for agriculture in the market

Table 3.6   Kazakstani gross agricultural production, 1990–93 (1990 = 100%)

	1990	*1991*	*1992*	*1993*
Agricultural output *including*	100	90.1	90.1	86.4
Livestock	100	96.0	87.9	45.5
Crops	100	81.0	93.7	150.8

Source: Table was calculated based on data from Selckoe/Selskoe, khozya'stvo Respubliki Kazakhstan, 1996.

economy, but the point was the defence of the national interests of the ethnic Kazak rural population. Before the movement to the market economy can be completed, it is necessary to solve the complicated inter-ethnic situation regarding the privatisation of land. The problem is that historically the ethnically Kazak peasantry has become pushed to non-irrigated and barren regions by the migration of non-nomadic settled agricultural (*zemledel' cheskikh*) peoples. It is obvious that the Kazak rural population did not wish to work for others on their historic land where, in the case of free sale of the land, they would not find it possible to purchase it. From this idea of national-patriotic support of the Kazak rural population, the concept of the national state system developed. In reality this 'game' was beneficial only for the bureaucracy, which considered only one solution of regulation of post-colonial and post-communist land contradictions.

> The Kazakh national bureaucracy, just like the Communists before them, while presenting themselves as the supporters and guardians of the interests of the impoverished native rural ethnics, are deceiving them one more time. In fact the 'home' bureaucracy merely makes worse the impoverished, 'feudal-routine' state of stagnation of rural Kazakhs, continuing to hold them back, and increasing their gap from historical progress. (Amrekulov and Masanov, 1994: 14).

LABOUR FORCES

In the period prior to transition, the population was paid wages and hired on the basis of central planning. In Kazakstan enterprises enjoyed incentives to employ more and more people, therefore labour shortage was the norm rather than 'unemployment'. The general figure of employed population in 1990 was 7 560 000 persons.

One of the major costs of the reforms has been surging unemployment, which did not exist, at least officially, under central planning. Available unemployment statistics for Kazakstan began to be collected only in the second half of 1991, after unemployment legislation became effective on 1 July 1991. So, it is impossible to estimate precisely the real economic trend from unemployment (Table 3.7).

Nevertheless, despite adverse developments in prices and output, employment remained reasonably stable in 1991, owing to a deliberate policy of protecting the labour forces of government or state owned enterprises. Wages declined in real terms as workers were only partially compensated for the April price adjustment. Further to liberalisation of prices,

Table 3.7   Unemployment in Kazakhstan, 1990–93

	1990	1991	1992	1993
Number of unemployed	–	–	33 681	40 514

Source: *Statisticheskii Yezhegodnik Kazkhstana*, 1995: 57.

the minimum wage in the public sector were raised by 90 per cent in mid-December 1991. The real wages declined by about one fifth.

The disenchantment of the population with the social consequences was increasing every year. But the government consistently tried to explain that all troubles were derived from Russia; that Kazakstan had to repeat all the steps of reforms introduced in Russia (prices liberalisation, wrong indexation). So, by 1993 the population was ready for the introduction of a new national currency as a universal panacea.

MONETARY POLICY AND PROBLEMS WITH THE ROUBLE ZONE

Kazakstani monetary policy was expected to be appropriately designed to reduce the severe inflation after the liberalisation of prices in January 1992. Prior to 1991, prices in the USSR were very stable. In 1990 the retail prices index was only 8.3 per cent higher than in 1985. The inflation of retail prices started to grow from the middle of 1991, but at a slower rate than wholesale prices. The notion of *liberalisation of prices* was understood only in one direction – that of increase. The recommendation of international organisations to develop prices rapidly to world relativities was a major mistake of the Union government because of its inflationary consequences and its redistributional consequences, that is, the adverse impact on those with fixed price incomes (workers, pensioners, civil servants, etc.), which was continued by the Kazakstani government. On 3 January 1992, a presidential decree stated that pricing will be established only through the balance of supply and demand. The rapid growth of inflation was caused by the lack of a systematic programme for the structural economic transformation, specifically, the arbitrary change of priorities during the economic transformation; non-systematic management; the blind application of foreign (western) policy prescriptions, misdirected and maladjusted investment policy, and the failure to complete plans and programmes.

By 1991, Kazakstan was a relatively small participant of the rouble zone, and had very limited control on monetary policy and inflation processes. At the same time, the National Bank of Kazakstan was unable to control the money supply. Of course it tried to regulate local demand via credit limits for the government and enterprises, and indirectly via interest rates. Kazakstan tried to follow Russian interest rates. Unfortunately, this monetary method was inefficient, because interest rates were negative when inflation is taken into consideration.

Required bank reserves were established at the beginning of 1991. At the beginning of 1992 they were increased to 18 per cent of deposits. In addition to this, banks had to keep correspondent accounts with the National Bank. Their main purpose was restriction of the growth of the money supply, cheap credit for the government, and the funding of credits of the National Bank of Kazakstan for refunding. By April 1992, such credits were near 60 per cent of all credits in the Kazakstani financial system. At this time, interest rates were eased, but were still under strict control. Compared with interest rates in Russia, interest rates in Kazakstan were artificially low.

The monetary policy of Kazakstan was formulated jointly with other participants of the rouble zone, particularly with Russia. The National Bank of Kazakstan tried to keep control on the volume of credit of the government and enterprises, and as a result, Kazakstan was faced with a lack of cash, and inter-enterprise arrears. Inter-enterprise arrears arise when firms that are owed money by their clients are in turn unable to pay their debts to their suppliers. Inter-enterprise arrears rose very rapidly from 1991, and one of the main reasons was a lack of ready cash. Another reason was the legacy of inter-enterprise arrears from the previous period. The phenomenon of inter-enterprise arrears is one of the main dangers for macroeconomic stabilisation during the transitional period, because '... these arrears would become so widespread that enterprises could use them as a substitute for money.' (Gros and Steinherr, 1995: 163). Therefore, it is possible to consider inter-enterprise arrears as an enterprise's way of making up a deficiency of working assets, with the aim of stabilising production.

'Suppliers' credit' is the same phenomenon as inter-enterprise arrears in developed market economies (Begg and Porters, 1992). Thus, the real question is whether growth in inter-enterprise arrears in transitional economies is of a similar nature to suppliers' credit[3] Simultaneously, the volume of barter increased rapidly and the demonetisation of the economy was intensified. From 1991, in the poor financial conditions, enterprises tried to provide at least a partial sale of their production. Pre payment became a necessary element for delivery.

Inter-enterprise arrears are credits for goods within the chain of production and distribution, and play the role of quasi-money. They lead to a further decline in production, as a result of the lack of finance for primary products and materials, and the failure of settling of debts between counteragents. Similar reasons may lead to inactivity, even to the extent of non-production. Later we will show how the problem of inter-enterprise arrears increased, and what the results were for the macroeconomics situation in Kazakstan. But even in 1991–92 it was obvious that inter-enterprise arrears were a persistent systematic phenomenon, and would self-feed on a larger and larger scale.

Of course Kazakstan cannot escape inflation, which arose in all countries of the former Soviet Union. After decades of stable prices, in 1991 consumer goods prices increased more than 150 per cent. Until the complete collapse of the rouble zone in August 1993, Kazakstan was a part of the very large currency zone, therefore in this period Kazakstan could not be responsible for the dynamic of prices and in general for changes in the rouble. It was not until after August 1993 that inflation become more of an internal problem for Kazakstan.

Until 1992 it was possible to regulate 'creeping inflation' by administrative means. Monetary expression of the increasing deficit of enterprises led to the occasional saving of financial resources in a whole country – particularly the deposit accounts of the population in *Sberbanks* (Saving Banks). There is no doubt that the badly prepared reform of prices in the former Soviet Union did not make enough effort towards stabilising the situation in 1991. The price reform at the beginning of 1992 (with correction of level of prices) partially liquidated the 'spare' money of the population. From August 1992 until August 1993, the main attention began to focus upon arresting the decline in production rather than halting inflation. Transfer in monetary expression of the large budget deficit in Russia and concentration upon purpose-specific credits helped to increase inflation, which was 25 per cent monthly.

From August 1993 until November 1993, when currency and the financial system was officially separated from Russia, inflation increased, as a result of the expansion of domestic (internal) credit as an answer to the request of enterprises, particularly agricultural enterprises. This has brought about the stopping of transfers to the corresponding accounts from Russia, thus cutting imports, which in turn reduced supply in conditions of increasing demand.

The hard monetary dependence of Kazakstan upon Moscow, as well as Russian policy pushing other former Soviet Republics from the rouble zone were leading Kazakstan to introduce a new national currency. Kazakstan tried until the last moment to normalise relations with Russia in this matter. On the one hand, the Kazakstani government understood that exit from the rouble zone would make a lot of trouble for them, because they would have to take all responsibility for macroeconomic stabilisation in the country, as well as providing the stability of a national currency. But on the other hand, the situation became worse in that state enterprises could not receive salaries within a certain time, and the Central Bank did not rush to provide a money supply for Kazakstan. From the beginning of 1993, the government started to create a strategy to introduce a new national currency.

THE PROGRAMME OF URGENT ANTI-CRISIS MEASURES AND THE PROMOTION OF SOCIO-ECONOMIC REFORMS (1993)

After independence, the government of Kazakstan introduced a set of reform programmes in order to dismantle central planning and move towards a market economy. The reformed economic structure and the stabilisation of the macroeconomic situation were major components of the reform programs. Kazakstan has chosen a different path towards 'marketisation' of production to many of the Former Soviet Republics. It is one which is far more gradual in approach, and one which attempts to avoid the pitfalls of the 'shock therapy' approach utilised in some neighboring economies. It is clear that the Kazakstani method was reactive as opposed to proactive during the post-independence period, in that there was not a specific blueprint for reform, rather that policy was formulated in reaction to events as they occurred.[4]

In the spring of 1993 after long debates and testing of different economic prescriptions President Nazarbayev and the Ninth Session of the Supreme Soviet of Kazakstan approved *The Programme of Urgent Anti-Crisis Measures and the Promotion of Socio-Economic Reforms*. The programme proposed a strong decrease in credit, and a large reduction in budget expenditure. The fiscal budget needed to be strongly controlled in order to compensate for the exclusion of large transfers, from the USSR in particular. The programme consisted of 11 parts:

- current economic situation;
- the main goals, problems and steps of implementation of this programme;
- structural and investment policy;
- financial and credit policy;
- policy of privatisation;
- development of entrepreneurship and anti-monopoly policy;
- system of social security;
- foreign economic policy;
- a crackdown on organised crime;
- *Perestroika* of executive organs of power and management; and
- mechanism of programme's realisation.

The aim of the programme is not clear. It is difficult to understand what is the final point of reform.

The given programme defines the plan of activity of the government in the 1993–1995 years. Its final aim is the creation of real market mechanisms and a socially-defined economy, conducted more independently and within the requirements of Kazakstan's national interests and policy, the entrance of the republic into the world economy, and on this basis the creation of conditions for improving standards of living. (*Kazakstanskaya Pravda*, 1993: 1)

All the objectives in the programme resemble slogans, and the methods of achieving them are not made clear. The public reasons for introducing this economic programme appeared primarily political as opposed to economic. The main argument was the collapse of the Soviet Union (!), and this after two years of Kazakstan's independence. The initial statements compel the reflection that the government of the country had lost its way in terms of economic management. 'During the last period the government *tried* to lead the course of decreasing of the sphere of state regulation of prices.' (*Kazakstanskaya Pravda*, 1993: 1). Nowhere is the reader informed about the results of these attempts. But it is very odd to only attempt the improving of the situation over *two* years. The impression from reading the programme is that the government still cannot understand the critical nature of the situation taking place throughout the country.

The programme was divided into three major steps:

1. *The first step (1993)* would solve the following problems: the reduction of inflation; halting the decline in industrial production, the creation of a base for growth of output in the medium term; changing the proportion of state and private sectors on the basis of privatisation of state ownership; softening of the negative consequences of transformation for vulnerable sectors of the population.
2. *The second step (1994)* includes the following priorities: institutional transformation; privatisation; the development of market infrastructure and a competitive market environment.
3. *The third step (1995)* aims to solve the key problem – the creation of regulatory mechanisms of the market economy on the basis of constructing a single and coherent policy in taxation, budget, prices, credit, investments, trade, labour and so on.

The main idea of this programme was 'to build our own policy, even integration with countries of CIS is very strong.' (*Kazakstanskaya Pravda*, 1993: 1). One of the main economic conditions, absolutely necessary for conducting the state's own policy, is to have a national currency. If we take into consideration this point, it is possible to note that in such conditions *The Programme of Urgent Anti-Crisis Measures and the Promoting of Socio-Economic Reforms (1993)* was unrealistic. The programme assumes that the possibility of introducing a national currency exists, but it is impossible to find in the programme the difference in the measures required for implementation of this programme in the rouble zone, and after a new national currency had been introduced. Obviously the timeframe suggested for the implementation of this policy was unrealistic. The monetary policy which the Kazakstani government proposed to conduct in the first period of reform was inappropriate, because the strong dependence in the rouble zone would restrict monetarist measures in Kazakstan. In the programme, the role of Russia in the monetarist fate of Kazakstan is unclear.

The policy of privatisation which was introduced in the programme is not precise. It is unclear how the government was supposed to manage this process. How the government is going to clarify the proportion of the ownership is problematic. Before this programme the privatisation programme was adopted, and it is impossible to find any links between existing and new programmes. There is practically no analysis of the first results of privatisation.

The deficit of the national budget was promised to be maintained at 3–5 per cent annually of GNP. These figures related to the situation in developed countries, but for Kazakstan's economy (which was in economic crisis) this appeared most optimistic.

The programme formulates the requirement that 'the satisfaction of the consumer market non-foodstuff products will be through the following measure: the introduction of protectionist measures to defend domestic production ...' (*Kazakstanskaya Pravda*, 1993: 1). It is very difficult to understand how these measures would help the population to acquire non-food products. The quality of the local production might be lower than that of imported goods, and this would not help to satisfy the consumer market.

In general, it is hard to fathom how these programmes were to be implemented, and it is unclear who would take responsibility (in the Kazakstani government) for their implementation. Therefore, by 1993, the Kazakstani government had a flawed guide for the conducting of the transformation of reforms.

4 The Introduction of the National Currency and the New Course of Reform

By the autumn of 1993[1] the Government of Kazakstan was faced with the very serious problem of the introduction of a new national currency. Although by some people it was considered a panacea for the crisis, generally the Kazakstani population realised that the real crisis was still in the future. The time for paying for independence would come soon, and in such a situation it would be impossible to blame the Russian or any other government for the unsuccessful method of transition. Nevertheless, the devaluation of the new national currency began very soon after its introduction, which of course demonstrated that the government was still very weak in terms of economic policy, and did not have clear and coherent relations with the National Bank of Kazakstan. The government was still uncertain as to what was necessary in terms of inter-enterprise arrears, and that it is necessary to conduct restructuring after a privatisation process.

The last (and the most peculiar) action was a governmental anti-crisis programme (July 1994), which was the last and clumsy attempt by government to change the economic situation. This programme remained more of a draft than the whole coherent concept of reforms, and again the slogan level of the programme reflected common features with the previous governmental economic programme.

NEW NATIONAL CURRENCY

On 15 November 1993, Kazakstan issued a new currency (Tenge) and left the rouble zone. The main aim of this was to give the Kazakstani authorities control over monetary policy, especially the rate of monetary emissions. The projects regarding the Tenge designed by national government were extremely optimistic, aimed at establishing the Tenge as a hard currency, recognised by other CIS countries and the rest of the world.

A number of motives slowed the full conversion to national currencies. In the absence of domestic macrostabilisation, it was almost certain that the new currencies would quickly lose value as a result of inflation – and their subsequent depreciation would undermine the political credibility of the new governments. (Economic Commission for Europe, 1993: 169).

The same thing had happened with the Tenge. The new national currency was 'stable' only during the first three weeks. The dynamic of the devaluation of Tenge is presented in Table 4.1.

In addition, the non-convertibility of the Tenge required partners of Kazakstani enterprises to make payments in hard currency, and this led to difficulties because of the calculation of inter-enterprise deliveries. As a consequence the use of barter was expanded, inter-enterprise arrears increased, and production continued to decline. Due to the rouble exchange rate with the Tenge, restrictions applied not only to individuals, but to institutions as well. An indefinite amount of money was frozen on the accounts.

In spite of the announced inter-governmental agreement regarding establishing transfer-payments, they were not carried out due to a lack of trust in partner-countries.

In Kazakstan from the middle of November 1993 to the middle of January 1994, the average monthly inflation was 50 per cent.

Table 4.1   Tenge auction rate

Date	Rate (Tenge/US$)	Volume (US$ million)	Change (%)
19.11.93	4.68	3.320	N.A.
03.12.93	5.70	7.835	21.8
27.1.94	9.35	N.A.	64.0
22.2.94	11.58	N.A.	23.8
31.3.94	19.94	13.310	72.2
28.4.94	29.92	15.390	50.0
31.5.94	40.73	10.965	36.1
30.6.94	43.29	8.385	6.28
28.7.94	45.33	6.825	4.71
29.9.94	48.00	10.100	5.89
27.10.94	49.55	9.485	3.23
29.11.94	51.20	12.975	3.33
29.12.94	54.26	11.520	5.98

Source: National Bank of Kazakstan, 1996.

THE EURASIAN UNION – A NEW INITIATIVE OF THE
KAZAKSTANI PRESIDENT

In the summer of 1994, President Nazarbayev came up with the idea of
establishing a new union of countries in Asia and Europe called the
Eurasian Union (Nazarbayev, 1994: 1–2). The concept of the Eurasian
Union was presented as another option in the reintegration of the CIS. By
that time all countries of CIS remained in political, economic, social and
cultural crises. The Eurasian Union might be a means to solve such a
difficult situation, and help the countries of CIS to find a new view on the
process of integration. The importance of such an alliance was emphasised
by President Nazarbayev in a meeting in Moscow State University and in
a public meeting with academics and journalists in Almaty, as a main
basis for rapid accord between CIS countries. This process would be much
quicker than the same process in the European Union, which had such a
possibility only after 40 years of existence.

The main difference between the CIS and the Eurasian Union lies in the
proposal of a joint Parliament, because one of the most important problems is the creation of a legislative base for conducting coherent economic
policy. Nevertheless, from our point of view it is possible to call the idea
of the Eurasian Union just as an improvement of the principle of the existing CIS concept.

A lot of people saw in the idea of the creation of the Eurasian Union an
attempt to revive the USSR. Supporters of President Nazarbayev argued
that the project of the Eurasian Union would ensure, through the creation
of the union of the independent states, maintaining the territories, political
sovereignty and other attributes which belong to the independent states.
All criticisms were interpreted as ignorant or based on a failure to understand the content of the project. Not all leaders of CIS countries came to
the meeting in Almaty, and in Moscow President Nazarbayev had a
limited audience in Moscow State University to introduce his project.
Official Moscow did not support this idea, and characterised the Eurasian
Union as a premature step. The real reasons of such opposing views lay in
the political and economic details of such a union. The first question
which arose was who will become the leader of the Eurasian Union. The
next painful problem was the unequal economic development of CIS
countries, which might create additional problems for partners in the
Eurasian Union. At that time it was unclear what kind of responsibilities
participants would have if there were some economic difficulties. The idea
of creating joint economic institutions such as the international investment
bank of the Eurasian Union, the commission for export of raw materials

from countries within the Eurasian Union, the commission of introducing
a calculated monetary unit (transfer rouble) and so on seems very open to
challenge. It was unclear how the role of each participant would be estimated, who would have more influence in the distribution of the funds, for
example from the international investment bank of the Eurasian Union.
One view was that through the idea of the Eurasian Union Kazakstan tried
to deal with its own economic crisis. It would not be true if we did not
recognise that in general the idea of the Eurasian Union had a rational
context, and the integration is a hugely important factor, but at the same
time all these actions were very premature. All the economies of CIS
countries were suffering serious difficulties and of course they would be
unable to design any rational union, which in reality could help the new
national economies. By that time economies were not created as
economies, for all countries the monetary problem was very complicated,
and the introduction of new national currencies (which was finished by
the end of 1993) did not help in the understanding of the introduction of
the transfer rouble of the Eurasian Union.

The main weakness of this programme was a poor economic explanation as to why such a union was really important at that time; how countries might gain from joint integration. The memory of the USSR
integration was still dominant for CIS states.

THE PROGRAMME OF GOVERNMENT ACTIVITY IN INCREASING REFORMS AND RECOVERY FROM THE ECONOMIC CRISIS (1994)

Loose fiscal and monetary policies spurred inflation, which increased by
over 1500 per cent in 1994. The situation was complex, and the Cabinet of
Ministers was absolutely unable to offer sufficient guidance. Nevertheless,
in July 1994 the government introduced a new *Programme of the
Government's Activity in Increasing Reforms and Recovery from the
Economic Crisis*. The programme covered all possible topics of reforms:
structural-investment policy, liberalisation of goods markets, creating conditions for economic growth, policy of competition and liberalisation of
prices, reduction of inflation, development of entrepreneurship, regional
policy, preparing human resources, foreign economic activity, and development of the housing market.

The new timetable (against that of the previous anti-crisis programme) for governmental activity was arbitrarily divided into three
periods:

1. *The first period (July–December 1994)*: The scenario of the development of reforms was supposed to be based on own resources and a minimum of borrowing external (foreign) resources, which would provide financing of budget deficits and balance of payments in volumes, which would be necessary for decreasing monthly inflation to a level lower than 10 per cent by the end of the year. At the same time it would consider some methods to stop the decline in production, which has an export character, involving loans required for improving reforms, stabilisation of the economy and realisation of the economic growth problems, and a strong social policy.

2. *The second period (January–September 1995)*: This is a period of transformation of the economy to the scenario of development, where the main element would be not the governmental restrictive financial policy for cutting budget deficit through the reducing of expenditures, but a course of leading anti-inflationary policy through the minimisation of growth in the budget deficit.

3. *The third period* in the governmental programme: Will involve a new economic course through the programme, which will be created to that time, the essence of which will be the continuation of a sharp anti-inflationary policy, stopping the decline in production and standards of living, and the creation of conditions for their growth.

What occurred in this programme was: the main aim of reforms: 'the main aim of medium term programme of governmental activity, following the purposes which were formulated in the June 1994 by Message of the President of Kazakstan, is an acceleration of economy's reforms and on this basis halting the decline in production and standard of living.' The main mistake of that period was that there was the desire on the part of decision makers to reform the economy, but unfortunately sometimes they followed the recommendation of international organisations (which tried to offer the standard package of reforms through the experience of the developing countries, where these reforms were unsuccessful sometimes, but the same package without taking into consideration the local specifics leads to increasing of negative effects in Kazakstan) or copying the programmes of Russian transformation. Very often Russian economic programmes were the main 'guides' during the preparation of the Kazakstani version of economic course. So, by the time the government took the course of halting inflation (the fact of correlation between inflation and non-payments in state owned enterprises – delays with wages' payments, inter-enterprise arrears – was still omitted), they still took into consideration the fact of the collapse of the Soviet Union (after 3 years!) and tried to explain the reforms as a result of structural distortions left by the previous regime. (See *Programme of Government's Activity of Increasing Reforms and Recovery from an Economic Crisis*, 1994).

The main dimensions of acceleration and improvement of reforms were reflected in part B of the programme, the most important being:

- structural investment policy;
- liberalisation of market goods;
- creation of conditions for economic growth;
- policy of competitiveness and liberalisation of prices;
- decreasing of inflation;
- development of entrepreneurship;
- foreign economic activity;
- regional policy;
- social policy;
- ecological policy; and
- preparation of human resources.

The impression which this programme left is that whilst the government was trying to improve the situation, unfortunately they could not build strong links between different parts of the reform programme. Each one of eleven parts is a separate programme of reform, and of course such a lack of links would not allow the achievement of a coherent result as a whole.

MULTI-SECTORAL CORPORATIONS AS A METHOD OF CREATING EFFECTIVE ECONOMIC STRUCTURES

From the beginning of the reforms, state enterprises faced problems such as the lack of supply of materials, technical know-how and sales. The situation often changed because the structure of demand was distorted, and there was a loss of value of savings and an increase in the volume of credit. Therefore, the financing of enterprises was changed, as well as its pricing. The enterprises tried to adapt to a new demand. But the specific features of adaptation were the opposite of expectations. The model of behaviour of enterprises was not adequate for market economy, and the results were barter, crisis of inter-enterprise arrears, etc. At the same time the model of managers behaviour started to be created, the main features of which were to keep enterprises solvent, and to find fish in the dirty water (see Box 4.1).

Box 4.1 The behaviour of Kazakstani large-scale enterprises

The phenomena of the behaviour of managers of large-scale enterprises which are partially still years under state control is very interesting. Previous works (Kalyuzhnova (1995/96a) Yanovskii (1996/97)) considered the model of survival of large-scale enterprises in transitional economies under rent-seeking management, which recently lost central planned control, but are still not in market conditions. This gives us the opportunity to conclude that Kazakstani enterprises are in exactly such a sort of situation. It is possible to describe the behaviour of these enterprises through the dynamic model where managers and local bureaucracy select from the large scale-enterprises a substantial number of small enterprises. As a rule the said small enterprises which have transferred to leased equipment tools, technology, and more skilled workers, creating on this basis joint-stock (daughter) small firms, or co-operatives are much more profitable. Because managers and local bureaucracy try to create a regime of the best conditions for these enterprises, they receive a percentage of the sales revenue of each small (daughter) firm. The receiving of profit by large scale enterprises sometimes is not a goal. The more important problem for managers of these enterprises is saving the position for daughter firms where they can obtain some personal benefit (see Figure 4.1).

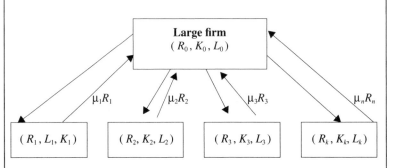

Figure 4.1 The set of small daughter firms

The mathematical presentation of the dynamic model which aims at maximisation of total manager's income and sales revenue of mother firm simultaneously, thus:

Maximise objective functional:

Box 4.1 Continued

$$J = \int_0^\infty \left(\alpha I(t) + (1-\alpha) R(t) \right) e^{-rt} dt \tag{1}$$

subject to

$$I(t) = W_M + \sum_{i=1}^k \mu_i R_i(t) + , \ O < \mu < 1 \tag{2}$$

$$R(t) = R_0(t) + \sum_{i=1}^k R_i(t), \ K = \sum_{i=0}^m K_i, \ L = \sum_{i=0}^m L_i \tag{3}$$

$$R_0(t) = W_M + W_w^0 L_0 + \delta_0 K_0 + K_0' + \pi_0 K_0 \tag{4}$$

$$(1-\mu_i)R_i(t) = W_w^i L_i + \delta_i K_i + K_i' + \pi_i(t)K_i, i = 1,2...m \tag{5}$$

$$W_M = \gamma \ K_0 + C_M L_0, \ o < \gamma < 1, \ o < \delta + \gamma < 1, \ C_M > O \tag{6}$$

where

$I(t)$	current manager's income
$R(t)$	sales revenue
P	price of a product
K	firm's capital
K_0	the capital of the large firm
K_i	capitals of small daughter's firms ($i = 1,2,...k$)
L_o	initial workers number of the large firm
L_i	initial workers number of small daughter firms
W_M	managers salary
W_w	average workers wage per one
L	number of workers
K'	net investment
C_M	coefficient of managers salary
π_c	the constraint for minimal profit or

π profit of shareholders if $\pi > o$ and losses, if $\pi > o$ per one worker

μ_i the managers sales revenue shares in i daughter's firm

γ the managers share of the firms capital K

$\delta, \delta, \dots \delta$ the rate of depreciation of capital K

r the positive rate of discount

α the weight coefficient; $0 \leq \alpha \leq 1$

Equation (2) describes the current income of managers. Equations (4) and (5) describe enterprises' expenditures and are for the creation of stocks for next business cycle. The manager's salary will depend on the size of capital and quantity of workers (see equation (6)).

For simplicity, suppose that the conditions of the main firm and daughter firms are closely connected each other. Suppose that during the time such notions as sale revenue, capital and number of workers of the main firm and daughter firms are coherent. That is to say:

$$R_i(t) = \beta_i R_0(t)$$
$$K_i(t) = \varepsilon_i K_0(t)$$
$$L_i(t) = \upsilon_i L_0(t); i = 1, 2, \dots, m, t \in (0, \infty) \tag{7}$$

In this case the problem (1)–(6) is transferred to the maximising functional:

$$J = \int_0^\infty \left(\alpha I(t) + (1-\alpha) R(t) \right) e^{-rt} dt \tag{8}$$

subject to $I(t) = W_M + \dfrac{\sum\limits_{i=1}^{k} \mu_i \beta_i R(t)}{1 + \sum\limits_{i=1}^{k} \beta_i}$, $O < \mu_i < 1, O < \beta_i < 1,$

$$O < \mu_i \beta < 1 \tag{9}$$

Box 4.1   Continued

$$W_M = \frac{\gamma}{1 - \sum_{i=1}^{m} \varepsilon_i} K + \frac{C_M}{1 - \sum_{i=1}^{m} \upsilon_i} L, o < \gamma < 1, o < \delta_0 + \gamma < 1, C_M > O,$$

$$(10)$$

$$\frac{R(t)}{1 - \sum_{i=1}^{m} \beta_i} = W_M + \frac{W_w L}{1 - \sum_{i=1}^{m} \upsilon_i} + \delta_0 \frac{K}{1 - \sum_{i=1}^{m} \varepsilon_i} + \frac{K'}{(1 - \sum_{i=1}^{m} \varepsilon_i)} +$$

$$\pi_0 \frac{K}{1 - \sum_{i=1}^{m} \varepsilon_i}$$

$$(11)$$

$$\frac{(1 - \mu_i)\beta_i R(t)}{1 - \sum_{i=1}^{m} \beta_i} = W_w + \frac{\upsilon_i}{(1 - \sum_{i=1}^{m} y_i)} L + \frac{\delta \varepsilon_i K}{1 - \sum_{i=1}^{m} \varepsilon_i} + \frac{\varepsilon_i K'}{(1 - \sum_{i=1}^{m} \varepsilon_i)} +$$

$$\frac{\pi_i \varepsilon_i K}{(1 - \sum_{i=1}^{m} \varepsilon_i)}$$

$$(12)$$

Deducting from equation (11) the sum of equation (12) we receive a system:

$$J = \int_{0}^{\infty} \left(\alpha I(t) + (1 - \alpha) R(t) \right) dt \qquad (13)$$

$$I(t) = W_M + \mu R(t) \qquad (14)$$

$$\mu = \frac{\sum_{i=1}^{m} \mu \beta_i}{1 + \sum_{i=1}^{m} \beta_i} \qquad (15)$$

$$W_M = \theta K + \tau L \tag{16}$$

where $\theta = \dfrac{\gamma}{1 - \displaystyle\sum_{i=1}^{m} \varepsilon_i}; \quad \tau = \dfrac{C_M}{1 - \displaystyle\sum_{i=1}^{m} \upsilon_i} \tag{17}$

$$(1 + S)R(t) = W_M + W_w L + \delta K + K' + \pi K \tag{18}$$

where $\delta = \dfrac{\delta_0 - \displaystyle\sum_{i=1}^{m} \delta_i \varepsilon_i}{1 - \displaystyle\sum_{i=1}^{m} \varepsilon_i} \tag{19}$

$$\pi = \dfrac{\pi_0 - \displaystyle\sum_{i=1}^{m} \pi \varepsilon_i}{1 - \displaystyle\sum_{i=1}^{m} \varepsilon_i} \tag{20}$$

$$S = \dfrac{\displaystyle\sum_{i=1}^{m} \mu_i \beta_i}{1 - \displaystyle\sum_{i=1}^{m} \beta_i} \tag{21}$$

We have a problem which was solved in equations (1, 2). If we denote $\kappa = \dfrac{K}{L}$ and suppose that $R(t) = PQ(t)$, $P > 0$; $Q = F(K, L)$ is the production function of aggregate of mother and daughters is the firms with K-aggregate capital, L-total number of workers. Then $F(K, L)$ is the homogeneous function is the of K, L variables, and it is possible to define:

$$\varphi(\frac{K}{L}) = Q(\frac{K}{L}, 1)$$

Let the function $\varphi(\kappa)$ have the following restrictions:
a) $\varphi'(\kappa) > 0$;   b) $\varphi''(\kappa) < 0$;   c) $\varphi'(\kappa) \to \infty$, for $\kappa \to 0$;   d) $\varphi'(\kappa) \to 0$, for $\kappa \to \infty$.

Box 4.1   Continued

From results (Kalyuzhnova Yanovskiy, 1995/96a, 1995/96b we have the existence of two equilibrium κ_1 (μ), κ_2 ($\alpha\mu$).

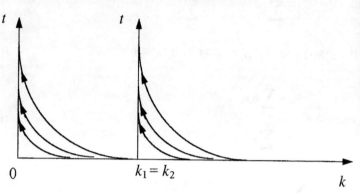

κ_1 (μ), κ_2 ($\alpha\mu$). are monotonic increasing functions with respect to μ. If an initial $\kappa_0 = \dfrac{K_0}{L_0}$ less than κ_1 (μ), then $k \to 0$ and the firm is collapsed.

In other cases the size of the firm is stabilised near κ_2 ($\alpha\mu$). We can consider κ_2 ($\alpha\mu$) as the optimal firm's size for given parameters above the function φ (k) of the transitional period. In the special case when $k_1 = k_2$ we have the following figure.

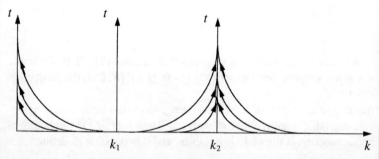

One can say the situation described by the model cannot continue a long time in Kazakstan, because it will lead to: (1) economic collapse and full bankruptcy of large – scale enterprises; (2) changes of monetary and credit policies to the additional monetary emission for solution of the problem of non-payments. Therefore it is necessary to provide a legislative base for shadow capital. At the present time this capital is leaving Kazakstan in different forms: purchases of properties in other countries, putting into personal accounts in the foreign banks, etc.

The situation was characterised by the following conditions: the structural-material imbalance of prices was very low for enterprises, but very high for the general population, which does not provide conditions for normal economic growth. At the same time enterprises which produced finished final goods faced the restrictions of solvent demand, because these enterprises first encountered the problem of the restriction of their demand in the conditions of the cost of growth. The problem was how was it possible to organise the work for enterprises in such transitional conditions? This situation was increasingly crucial as the process of privatisation and the creation of a commercial sector took place, which tried to monopolise the sphere of production.

Taking into consideration all the conditions of the transitional period, the process of transformation involved the concept of corporatisation, which allowed the uniting of the industrial resources of enterprises for the realisation of major projects. The factors which support and enhance the advantages of this from the economic point of view are:

- the management of the economy will increase in the due course of corporatisation;
- the provision of more opportunities for concentration of capital at the most important dimensions of the economy;
- the creation of conditions for diversification of production;
- the expansion of opportunities of support for small and medium size enterprises, which have unstable conditions;
- the expansion of small private business.

and from the enterprise level:

- the opportunity to stabilise the work within market conditions, through the concentration of capital and the creation of conditions for quick movement of capital in profitable spheres of production;
- the expansion of the volume of profit through the scale of production and size of capital fixed on the world market;
- the reduction of the costs of production and circulation through increasing the scale of production and centralising of the system of deliveries and sales;
- the fixing of already existing production links and easy creation of new ones;
- the establishment of proper relations with banks through creating links with already existing banks or founding of their own banks; and
- the attempt to make production attractive.

Corporations would take the lead in the decentralisation of management of the economy. Step by step the increasing growth in the size of corporations will help to increase the size of savings and the degree of concentration of capital in the most effective way. All these measures will lead to a reduction in the regulation of the economy by the government. Otherwise, decentralisation will mean chaos and anarchy, which will be brought about by small producers. The creation of large corporations would not contradict the processes of creating small private entrepreneurs. In Kazakstan most small and immediate size businesses were engaged in commerce. This is due to a lack of size of private capital, high inflation and quick losses in the value of savings as well as the high speed of capital turnover in commerce.

The advantages of large corporations, from the enterprise point of view, is easy access to credits and governmental support, because of a large and permanent influence on the process of production as well as the size of financial operations. The large industrial unit has a large scope of market, therefore 'smoothing over' of concerns in the local market takes place in order to increase the stability of sizes of profit, to the benefit of enterprises. Size of financial capital gives more stability in financial terms. Corporations will have economy on production costs, because of the scale of production, as well as with costs of sale and delivery. Corporations with the help of constant high investment are able to create different types of products, which will decrease the level of dependence upon the market, and expand areas of implications. All these advantages were clear to enterprises. By November 1992 in Kazakstan 330 enterprises had been transformed into joint-stock companies with total authorised fund of 14 641.7 million roubles. In comparison with developed countries, the corporatisation in Kazakstan had some specific features which were dictated by the current transitional conditions. First of all this was the high level of concentration and monopolisation of production existing on the branch level market of enterprises – especially on the basis of monopolist enterprise's branches. Secondly, the creation of a large number of formal corporations on the basis of which were attempts by former ministries and departments to save their position in the structure of economic management. These corporations of branch types, which were created by 'vertical dependence' were very often artificial. Thirdly, the weakness of the developing stock market and dominance of closed and semi-closed joint stock companies with limited movement of security, constituted a barrier for the formation of a system of free transfer capital through branches, and the attractiveness of free resources of population to production. The securities market was completely undeveloped. For example, from all share issues in transformed enterprises, only 2.1–2.2 per cent, of the total amount was sold.

All these specific features influenced the corporatisation of the economy. The corporatisation had a narrow and specialised character, and was based upon a certain degree of monopolisation of production. All these factors meant that corporatised enterprises would not have a level of stability in the conditions of the structural crisis and sharp changes of demand.

The question was what kind of corporations were *needed* by Kazakstan, and what kind of corporations were *created* in Kazakstan? Many people saw in the rising of multi-sectoral corporations (20–30 corporations) through the example of South Korea the method to create a skeleton of a new Kazakstani economy. This process would be a state initiative. But the programme of such activity was supposed to remove the state from direct involvement in the economy, and therefore the result was the creation of holdings.

In the initial stages of independence, the economy of the republic needed diverse industrial structures which would allow free and unhindered transfer of capital from one branch (of industry) to another. The obvious form of corporatisation was big corporations with high diversity of production. However, in Kazakstan department branch corporations (concerns) were created which did not have this diversity, rather having a very specialised focus of production. The problem with monopoly in raw material sectors made it impossible to create large diversified corporations. For example, many types of industrial goods were produced solely by one, two or three enterprises (tractors (1 producer), fabrics (2), and so on). Production of ferrous metals was concentrated in the Karaganda Metallurgical Combinat. Of course, this restricted horizontal integration, and the weakness of the enterprise's investment base was not conducive to the creation of diversification in production. The opportunity was to create highly diversified corporations on the basis of general technology of production and sale through the united republican concerns with appropriate enterprises in other CIS countries (the principle of trans-national corporations). Nevertheless, during the period some corporations were created (outside the production sphere) which had quite substantial financial resources and links of trade-financial sub-departments. However, at the same time they did not have a substantial production base.

The policy of privatisation, a mistaken definition of 'monopoly', and bias (prejudice) against large-scale enterprises were reasons for the state policy regarding liquidation of such economic units. Restructuring of the economy became liquidation of such economic forms. An example of this is the history of the KRAMDS, the company which was established, peaked, and subsequently collapsed (see Box 4.2).

Box 4.2   History of KRAMDS – national joint-stock company

KRAMDS Company was ranked among the first market structures of the former USSR and was incorporated under Number 1 in the Kazakstan Republican Association for Inter-industry Business Co-operation.

Later it was transformed into a national joint-stock company, according to the Decree of the President of the Republic of Kazakstan on 21 June 1993, which was developing, and raising its Statutory Fund (700 000 000.00 Tenge).

In 1993 the amalgamation of private capital of KRAMDS corporation with the state capital of KRAMDS corporation in the form of stocks of 37 large enterprises in different sectors of industry took place. The transformation of the system, inclusion of new plants, factories and sectors companies into the united infrastructure was aimed to provide fast and deserved access of the company's high quality produce and services to domestic and international market.

At the beginning of 1994 the specific volume of sectoral companies, plants and factories of KRAMDS national joint-stock company in the total output of Kazakstan was equivalent to 3.58 per cent, corresponding to sectors shown in Figure 4.2.

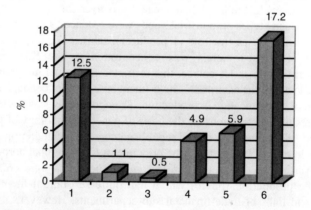

1. Ferrous metallurgy
2. Non-ferrous metallurgy
3. Chemical industry
4. Machine building
5. Construction materials
6. Light industry

Figure 4.2   Shares of KRAMDS in sectors of National Economy 1994 (figures from KRAMDS corporation)

From the outset, the plans of KRAMDS were most ambitious. In practice the achievements were much more moderate: even the president of KRAMDS, Victor Tyo, in his interview to the newspaper 'Express-K' Nurushin 1994: 3) said that for the successful restructuring of all 37 state-owned enterprises which were transferred to KRAMDS by President Nazarbayev's Decree, US $500million would be necessary. KRAMDS did not have such money for investment, and of course they needed governmental support (as credits, of governmental guaranties, for foreign credits, which KRAMDS could receive), but they could only start from own abilities. They did have intellectual resources and a unique structure of corporation. It is necessary to recognise that KRAMDS had readily very qualified people (a lot of former directors of large-scale enterprises, high profile industrial specialists, who knew production very precisely), and the existing management structure of the corporation was also impressive, but nevertheless, the problem of real money was still important. It is possible to argue this point at length, regarding the weight of KRAMDS in the developing of the Kazakstani economy, but the most demonstrative fact in this debate might be the statistics from that time, which were produced by KRAMDS themselves (Table 4.2).

So, by 1993–94 KRAMDS had invested approximately US$3 million, because some of the state-owned enterprises needed substantial amount of investment for recovery. KRAMDS, as other Industrial Financial Groups (IFG) needed governmental support, such as direct investments or governmental guaranties, or at least an expression of moral support or confidence. Privatisation was not real privatisation, because on the one hand KRAMDS could not consider itself a real owner (due to the political games of Cabinet Ministers), on the other hand KRAMDS would be unable in transitional conditions to produce enough financial resources for economic restructuring. One of the positive aspects of KRAMDS' activity was the existence of investment projects which might be implemented in good circumstances. These investment projects were created by KRAMDS, and were concerned with creating some holdings such as KRAMDS-Khromit, KRAMDS-Munaigas, etc. It would be possible to reanimate a lot of sectors of the economy. The question which arose is why the government, which transferred 37 enterprises under the KRAMDS' jurisdiction', was behaving as if it was some game: yesterday – transferred enterprises, today – decided to bring them back. The state still had shares in these enterprises, in other words it was the owner of these enterprises. All these intrigues by some of the members of the state elite resulted in a negative influence upon the conditions of enterprises. Eventually the Government made the decision about reorganisation of

Box 4.2 Continued

Table 4.2 Investment of KRAMDS corporation, 1993–94

N	Enterprises	Currency	Total amount
1	Kombinat of silk materials. (Ust-Kamenogorsk).Artificial fur production line	US$'000	800.0
2	Joint-Stock Company ' Dzhambultricotazh'. (Fabric) (Dzhambul). Fabric production line	Tenge '000	2 500.0
3	Joint stock company KRAMDS-LEGPROM (Almaty).Fabric production line	US$'000	70.0
4	Kazakstani-Turkish joint company 'KRAMDS-Talrandzhilar'. Sewing department, maintenance of leather-processing equipment, construction of sewage facilities	US$'000	1 140.0 (KRAMDS) 398.0 (Turkey)
5	KRAMDS-APK SADAVOD, (Chilik district, Almaty oblast). Vegetable store with refrigerator for 500 tonnes	Tenge '000	170.0
6	Joint Stock Company KRAMDS-SELKHOZTEKHPROM JSC. Department for production of medicinal produce from animals	Tenge '000	100.0
7	Constricting Broiler Poultry Factory, (Atyrau), KRAMDS-SELKHOZTEKHPROM JSC. For 500 thousand head	Tenge '000	5 000.0
8	'Al'batek' (Almaty). Medical herbs production line	Tenge '000	102.5

Source: B.

structure of the economy as a privatisation and structural Perestroika. The government produced Resolution N1671 'Questions National Auction Company KRAMDS' (6.12.1995) and KRAMDS was liquidated. In terms of welfare who lost, who won? Obviously some of members of the state elite found personal benefit from KRAMDS' liquidation, but at least enterprises were again put on the card table of redistribution of Kazakstani property. On the other hand the national economy lost a real opportunity to reanimate.

The KRAMDS corporation was a unique possibility to consolidate the efforts in the industrial sphere in the transition period. The wish by the ruling elite to create an ethnic national bourgeois instead of a multiethnic environment was the reason which stopped the process of corporatisation as a whole. Priority was given to the new national companies, the leaders of which were the young Kazak generation. As a rule they did not have any experience in the industrial sphere, but had a lot of patriotic rhetoric about the development of the Kazakstani economy. Usually they actively participated in the trade and re-sales, received enormous amount of governmental credits,[2] assisted the President in public forums and meetings with people, promoted themselves both widely and loudly and tried to participate in the decision-making process.[3] The main dangers of this process for the national economy was that these companies were operated only on a credit basis and did not have their own capital, valuable for the development production sphere. But at the same time it was quite convenient for the ruling elite because such a new bourgeois class would be unable to present any substantial opposition and was totally dependent upon them.

III

Privatisation and Structural Reforms in the Industrial Sector

5 Privatisation

The process of privatisation is not an easy one for any country, and this process is particularly difficult in a period of transition. When the state form of ownership has existed for a long time the difficulties with transformation include changing the fundamental ethos of the population as a whole, as well as the adoption of the key principles of private ownership (by the state).

Privatisation in Kazakstan began at the beginning of the period of transition, but during the period of implementation the Kazakstani government made a number of substantial and important conceptual errors. The consequences of adopting the wrong process for privatisation are reflected in the industrial sector in production and in further decline in output.

The methods with which the Kazakstani government tried to solve state financial problems and transfer control of enterprises to foreign companies would not necessarily lead to the stabilisation of the economy, and may even have wider socio-economic implications.

EXPLAINING PRIVATISATION IN TERMS OF ECONOMIC INTERESTS

Most sources accept that privatisation started in 1992, but in reality the Privatisation and Denationalisation Act of June 1991 was the starting point in the transformation of property rights. However, the government of Kazakstan started *seriously* working on a privatisation program in 1992. Subsequent legislation has been influenced by the rent-seeking behaviour of various socio-economic groups – entrepreneurs, bureaucrats, etc. In the process of privatisation, over a half of all enterprises were sold through auctions and commercial competitions. Kazakstan's new constitution prohibits private ownership of land, but long-term leasing with the right of inheritance is permitted.

Privatisation of public enterprises represents an important package of measures achievable by institutional and systematic transformation. The methods, forms and scale of the implementation of privatisation are the keys to a systematic transformation of the national economy and society as a whole.

It is almost impossible to distinguish between the political and economic aspects of privatisation, since economic policy is not only influenced to a great extent by political events that take place, but is indeed defined by these events, as most if not all of the decision making power is in the hands of politicians.

From an economic point of view, the main purposes of this process are:

- to increase the efficiency of the economy, and the competitiveness in internal and external markets;
- to create a private sector in the economy;
- to provide investment inflow and financial resources to the production sphere and its stabilisation;
- to reduce the public sector borrowing requirement and thus reduce budget deficit.

Privatisation does not necessarily lead to success and high economic growth in all cases. In some state industries, however, the desired results have been achieved. Certainly privatisation is necessary, but it is not sufficient for creating an effective market economy. In other words, privatisation is not good for the economy if the methods and forms in which it is done have only political and ideological purposes. In addition, the process of privatisation does not have the support of the required legislative base in Kazakstan.

The notion 'interest' may be used for explanation of economic situations as well as political problems. The method of estimation of the process of the development of macroeconomic policy is based on the term 'national economic interests'. National interests are reflected in the state and legislative laws.

If we turn to the etymology of the word 'interest', we shall discover that this is the notion which characterises something objectively important, significant for people, nation, state. Interest is the result of objective social conditions, which define certain will orientation and peoples' activity. Unfortunately, there is no distinct definition of national interests in economic science at the present time. This has to a certain degree influenced the fast development of social-political and economical processes in the former USSR which led to its decay. But we could see national economic interests as a bundle of the interests of social groups.

In Kazakstan the first and most important problem is the establishment of national interests, and the working out of a long-term strategy to protect and maintain these interests. Long-term economic aims have to be a priority and the achievement of all practical and short-term aims for the stabilisation of the economy must not override the main objectives.

It can be argued that all measures have to be appraised in priority not only from the point of view of the immediate stabilisation of the social-economic situation of the Republic, but also taking into account their long-term effect. Development for Kazakstan is the creation of a structure for the economy, the functioning of which will provide growth of GNP (as a criterion of welfare). To the extent that economic agents may subconsciously start to translate each others desires. Thus in the conditions of transitional economy it is important for the government to shape the interests of various groups towards a certain general economic interest, associated with the nation's well-being.

National interests are a complex system of numerous purposes, aspirations and activities which are directed towards the formulation and protection of the domestic and foreign objectives of the country. Generally speaking, national interests have never expressed the interests of all the people. I therefore begin by setting out the interests of every group in Kazakstan. These groups and their relationships to one another are shown in Figure 5.1.

The question which naturally arises from the above is how to get from a groups welfare to a set of criteria of social (general) choice without interpersonal comparisons. The main difficulty is in deciding upon a course of action that will maximise the utility of different groups. The interests these groups had in the process of re-structuralisation in a transitional economy was that of influential groups being able to affect the final outcome favourably to themselves and not taking into account the interests of other groups. This may well be Pareto inefficient as in some cases a rise in the well-being of one group will occur at the same time as a fall in the well-being of another group (using ordinal rankings only). It is no revelation that government expression of economic interest can lead to inefficiency of resource use in markets, or that the higher the rents transferred by such policies, the more tenacious the defence of such action will become.

Entrepreneurs express their personal interests, and exert pressure on government. 'The business character of the pressure system is shown by almost every list available' (Schattschneider, 1960: 31). This high degree of corporation among entrepreneurs is particularly significant in view of the fact that most other groups are inadequately organised. They unite in lobby groups, which conduct a policy of maximum preferences for the development of entrepreneurship. They demand tax free periods; changes in the export-import policy (removal or establishment of trade barriers); changes and establishment of new laws according to their own personal needs; opportunity to influence the establishment of priority directions in the development of national economy (as we can see, this case demonstrates the substitution of national interests for group interests).

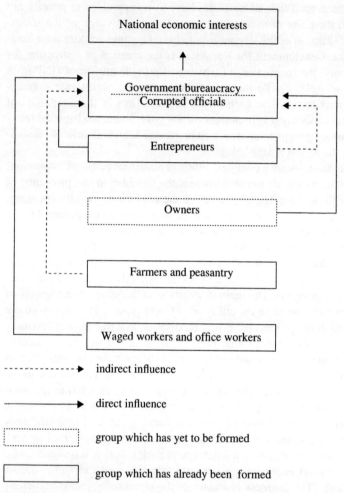

Figure 5.1 Creation of national economic interests in Kazakstan

Entrepreneurs involve members of government (indirectly or directly) in the sphere of business, transforming personal interests of entrepreneurs into the interests of *Government bureaucracy*.

Owners: although the concept of private property and therefore of ownership exists in contemporary Kazakstan, the exact role of owners is at present unclear. Defining an 'owner' broadly as one who has ownership (that is the capacity to receive profit from an object, which exists as a property) then the owner of an economic resource can be identified by the exercise of the control of the allocation and the receipt of profit from it. We can suppose that members of this group would speak in support of a proposal designed to create private ownership of economic durables (i.e. ownership of land, industrial and agricultural enterprises, financial organisations and so on). Also problematic are legislative aspects, which are under the influence of state 'government bureaucracy' and 'corrupted officials'.

Farmers: this group would have been connected with owners, if they had an opportunity to attract the attention of the decision makers to their problems. However, from 1930 the peasantry had no chance to express their interests, because these interests were influenced exogenously (e.g. the case with collectivisation in USSR). This tradition has influenced the present situation in peasantry, whose interests were overridden by the interests of other groups. In other words, as a consequence the farmers became non-coherent in their opinions and needs and were unable to express their interests. This could be explained by distortions in government policy concerning the social position of peasantry, for example, for a long time in the former USSR they did not receive their wages in monetary terms. All this caused a change in the awareness of their own interests.

Farmers influence 'government bureaucracy' in an indirect way (personal connections, blood relations etc.).

Waged workers and office workers: undoubtedly this group has experience of expressing their interests. They influence *government bureaucracy*, but this influence is strictly limited. Linking with or transforming into other groups is practically impossible, because *waged workers* have a traditional way of life (the urban way). Therefore the transformation to *farmers and peasantry* will be incredibly difficult; *waged workers and office workers* cannot afford to become *owners*, simply because of low wages. Whereas *entrepreneurs* would try and create various entry barriers, this group would have to be small, so a common dependence and a pressure for conforming behaviour emerges which may lead to an agreement for joint activity. Thus entry for *waged workers and office workers* would be more difficult. Their interests are the expression of the interests of a medium level of society: higher wages; improved working and social conditions; provision of pensions, better health services and so on.

Governmental interests are the interests of the ruling elite, although they can also be described as national interests. National interests can be defined as the interests expressing objective necessities of the whole society. Kazakstan's national interests lie first of all in the sphere of the domestic economy – it is necessary to feed the people.

We think it possible to distinguish as a group *government bureaucracy* (including *corrupted officials*), because the creation of state interests

(interests of the elite, which after a transformation and formulation become state interests) takes place at these levels. However, 'if the bureaucracy devises bad rules, norms, and reward systems and intervenes counterproductively, it harms economic performance.' (Gregory, 1990: 5). We need to make this distinction because of the extent of its influence on the economy. The existence of corrupted officials is recognised not only unofficially, but also mentioned in several speeches by the President of Kazakstan.

We assume that bureaucrats attempt to maximise their own utility and are not directly interested in the official purpose of the organisation.

Naturally the real purpose of bureaucrats is to increase their own power, scale of prestige and income. These elements are closely connected with hierarchical position in a formal organisation. This approach to the analysis of the bureaucracy has some analogy with the price system. The bureaucrat is subject to similar constraints to those working in the market as he deals with people whose interests are affected by the decisions he or she takes. He therefore becomes acquainted with costs and benefits, that is, there is an invisible hand governing bureaucratic behaviour.

State interests are group interests, made up of principles and views borrowed from other groups' interests. This is closely related to the theory of rent-seeking. This issue comes into effect when the efforts of various interest groups to get a monopoly position are socially wasteful. Buchanan (1985) has identified three different types of socially wasteful aspects of rent seeking behaviour. The efforts and expenditures of the potential recipients of the monopoly and the efforts of government officials to obtain the expenditures of potential recipients are especially applicable to transitional economies.

THREE PHASES OF KAZAKSTANI PRIVATISATION

In the process of privatisation in Kazakstan over a half of all enterprises were sold through auctions and commercial competitions. These methods of privatisation were most common in retail, public catering and consumer services (over 90 per cent of privatised enterprises), saunas and launderettes (practically all these).

The creation of joint-stock companies of both 'opened' and 'closed' types has become the most dominant way of privatising state enterprises in industry, construction, transport and wholesale trade. Over 80 per cent of industrial, 75 per cent of transport, 66 per cent of construction enterprises and over half of wholesale enterprises were privatised through joint-stock companies.

According to Kazakstani experts, the effectiveness of the sale of lots in 1995 was lower than that of 1994 for the following reasons: first, there was an element of novelty in 1994; secondly, the population's ability to pay had fallen in the middle of 1994; and thirdly, the best enterprises were offered for sale in 1994, whereas in 1995 it was only the remains that were left.

To examine the consequences of privatisation we must regard privatisation from the point of view of the national economic interest. There will be a negative influence on privatised enterprises such as violation of the procedure of control, carrying out partial auctions and so on. All these facts illustrate the participation of the decision makers in the process of the realisation of their personal economic interests through the transformation of share of property.

The results of *Phase 1 (1991–92)* of privatisation are therefore that 'farmers', 'peasantry', 'waged workers' and 'office workers' were disappointed by the economic meaning of the process of privatisation. This was because the coupon mechanism and privatising of housing did not bring the expected result. Entitlement to the coupons was determined according to a formula devised to provide for a citizen who has worked for 21 years; there were coupons sufficient to purchase an average flat. Additional coupons were given to parents, children, meritorious workers and certain others. The Decision by Privatisation Law (Decision) also provides a formula for valuation of houses as of the date of the Decision. Whilst the Act permits the coupons to be used to purchase any state property to be privatised, the Decision limits the use of coupons to Phase 1 privatisation left over from the sale of houses, small shops and small enterprises. The population kept a part of the coupons after the privatisation of housing, and they were supposed to use them for purchasing state property in *Phase 2 (1993–95)*.

The system of investment privatisation coupons was established for mass privatisation, and therefore housing coupons lost their validity. Every citizen of Kazakstan has the right to receive a 'personal voucher coupon book' (1993 (end)–1994 (January)). The problem of the allocation of voucher coupon books is a complex one because Kazakstan is one of the largest areas of the CIS and the population is very unequally distributed. Over 95 per cent of the population received 'personal voucher coupon books', which consist of 10 cheques, each cheque being worth 10 coupons, that is, there are 100 coupons in the 'book'. Citizens of agricultural regions receive 12 cheques, that is, 120 coupons. Citizens have to put their coupons into Investment Privatisation Funds (IPF), which are the official intermediaries between citizens and enterprises which are to be privatised. The purpose of IPFs is for investing coupons in enterprises, and citizens will become shareholders with the help of IPFs. In auctions held by the State Property Committee (SPC), investment privatisation coupons are exchanged for shares. Initially 51 per cent of shares were intended to be auctioned, 10 per cent to be given to the staff and 39 per cent to the state.

According to the Chairman of the State Property Committee at the time (Mr S. Kalmurzayev) it followed that on 1 January 1995, 33 per cent of the investment coupons had been used by the population (Figure 5.2).

The population was not in any hurry to put investment coupons into Investment Privatisation Funds, because it was very difficult to determine the realistic opportunity of being an owner. Even 'entrepreneurs' were very doubtful of the value of investment coupons.

The concept of privatisation through investment privatisation coupons was a mistaken one, as 'free' privatisation is untenable. At the present time the situation in Kazakstan with regards to investment privatisation coupons is unclear. Logically, if such privatisation continues, privatised enterprises (which received coupons instead of money) will become bankrupt, or investment privatisation funds will be unable to pay dividends to their investors.

The geography of mass privatisation also has systematic characteristics. This was expressed through the number of privatised enterprises in economically developed oblast (regions) for example, Shimkent and Karaganda oblasts, whereas Taldy-Korgan and Arkalyk oblasts were very much less involved in the process of mass privatisation.

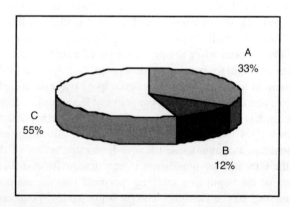

A – share of used coupons in relation to the total amount (33%)
B – share of unused coupons in relation to the total amount (12%)
C – share of coupons not transferred to Investment Privatisation Funds (55%)

Figure 5.2 The proportion of used coupons to total amount of coupons given out to the population of Kazakstan

The government of Kazakstan started working on the programme of privatisation on the basis of its own projects in 1993, after a law which gave the government the right to sell 49 per cent of the shares of the Almaty Tobacco Factory (this is the only tobacco enterprise in Kazakstan).

In November 1993 the government of Kazakstan decided to organise the privatisation on the basis of their own projects – the sale of the shares of Shimkent Confectionery Factory and Margarine Plants in Almaty and Karaganda. These three pioneering privatisation projects created a structural base for the program of privatisation based upon the government's own projects.

The following enterprises were privatised during the first step:

1. Almaty Tobacco Factory: 49 per cent of shares were sold to Philip Morris Company for US$ 313 million (US$ for cash and investments).
2. Shimkent Confectionery Factory: 90 per cent of shares were sold to RJR Nabisco for US$ 70 million (US$ for cash and investments).
3. Margarine Plants (Almaty and Karaganda): 90 per cent of shares were sold to Unilever for US$ 60 million (US$ for cash and investments).

In 1994 the Kazakstani government chose 110 enterprises to be privatised according to their own governmental projects. A tender for the right to become an adviser of the State Property Committee (SPC) between consulting firms was announced, which was the usual procedure followed by SPC when working on privatisation projects. In 1995 SPC was planning to privatise an additional 72 enterprises on the basis of their own projects.

According to the legislative base needed to create suitable conditions for privatisation, we can remark that the government of Kazakstan started working on a privatisation program in 1992. Since then there have been a lot of laws and acts concerning privatisation, property etc. published ('National Programme of Denationalisation and Privatisation 1993–1995', 'About Transferral of Ownership of State Farms to the Directors', 'About Sale of State Agricultural enterprises to the Public', 'About the Procedure of auctioning of State Enterprises and Sale of State Packages of Shares within Small-Privatisation' and so on). The main disadvantages of all these documents was a lack of logic of reform of property, a shortage of elements of market infrastructure; mass-scale denationalisation of economy and mass-scale of privatisation of state property are taking place in conditions of economic slump, decreasing of investment activity, etc. Therefore it will be necessary to create a new *concept of privatisation*, which must include all the lessons from the privatisation of previous period.

In 1995 Kazakstan began a new programme of privatisation which was *Phase 3 (1996–98)* in the process of privatisation. This third phase is the phase of privatisation through the individual projects.

The *Financial Times* called the Kazakstani privatisation 'Kazakstani sale of the century' (*Financial Times*, 25 October 1996): 'Speed differentiates Kazakhstan's [*sic*] privatisation more than anything. One company asked a consultancy to submit a proposal for a three week legal and commercial investigation for a bid. Two days later the consultancy found out that the company had already won the bid.' In addition to the concern over the speed of some of the sales, there also is a question mark over the role of corruption in the sale process. The government portrays this as a positive process, but foreign investors, the mass media and the ordinary population remain in a position of uncertainty: 'The motherland is selling very quickly, recklessly and for a trifle. Perhaps the reason is mercenary interests of the corrupted bureaucracy.' (*Panorama*, 1996 N 45). Table 5.1 provides details of some of the state enterprise sales.

AN EVALUATION OF PRIVATISATION

Privatisation as an element of economic system can be regarded as one of many national economic interests.

Table 5.2 illustrates that only three sectors of the Kazakstani economy were intensively privatised during 1992–94 (trade 26.3 per cent, consumer service 17.5 per cent, and agriculture 14.6 per cent).

Table 5.2 also illustrates that the *active* process of privatisation in agriculture (1992–95) had slowed down significantly in 1996, and in this case it is correct to associate the slowing down of the process with the completion of this sectoral privatisation. The situation in industry is *vice versa*: in that by 1992 only 211 enterprises were privatised, then 437 enterprises were privatised in 1996. An exception was 1995 (where there were only 48 industrial enterprises privatised), because by that year new types of privatisation, such as money privatisation, were introduced.

The accepted model of privatisation in Kazakstan cannot solve the problems involved in promoting investment in the development of the means of production, and in particular in mobilising the savings of the general population for the investment tool purposes. The reason for this is that the privatisation model is based upon purely political principles, and attempts to keep the principle of social justice and the creation of equal opportunities for all the population through their participation in the process of property redistribution. 'In mercantile society, therefore, more is required

Table 5.1 Details of state enterprise sales

Title of enterprise	Date of sale	Basis of sale (assets or package of shares in %)	Firm-buyer	Debts payable (Tenge million)[a]	Debts receivable (Tenge, million)[e]	Investment (US$ million) million	Bonus (US$ million)	Value of agreement total[b]
1	2	3	4	5	6	7	8	9
Ispat-Karmet (State share enterprise Karaganda Metallurgic Combinate)	15.11.95	Assets	Ispat-International	28 280	11 719.8	450	225	838.6[c]
Pavlodar Alluminium Plant	14.09.95	50 1.5 – public shares	Whiteswan Ltd	1 937.0	1 618.2	123	22.1	169.6[d]
TNK Kazchrom including:	15.10.95	52 3.2 public shares, 2 IPF	Japan-Chrome Corp.			398	66.8	582.59
a) Joint Stock (AO) Akssuskii plant of ferrosplav (AO Ermakovkii plant) b) AO				6 926.64	2 771.68	125		186.09
Ferrochrom (AO Aktyubinskii plant ferroslpuv)	15.10.95		Japan-Chrome Corp.	1 010	1 288.9	15		61.32[e]

Table 5.1 (Cont.)

Title of enterprise	Date of sale	Basis of sale (assets or package of shares in %)	Firm-buyer	Debts payable (Tenge million)[a]	Debts receivable (Tenge, million)[e]	Investment (US$ million) million	Bonus (US$ million)	Value of agreement total[b]
1	2	3	4	5	6	7	8	9
c) AO Donskoi Gok	15.10.95		Japan-Chrome Corp.	544.2	558.8	258		268.38
AO Torgaiskoe boksitovoe rudoupravlenie	5.04.96	51	Whiteswan Ltd	703.3	283.7	10.5	2.68	13.18
AO Krasnootyabrskoe boksitovoe rudoupravlenie	5.04.96	51 Ltd	Whiteswan	592.9	130.8	20.5	8.66	29.16
AO Keregitas	5.04.96	51	Whiteswan Ltd	655.7		19.0	0.66	19.66
AO Sokolovo-Sarbaiskoe GOPO	13.02.96	49 1.5 – public shares	Aivedon International	2 173.0	3 263.0	56	48.86	124.7[f]
AO Zheskazgan Svetmet	24.05.96	40 5 IPF	Samsung Dochland GMBKH	13 500	8 871	302	49.2	351.2

Table 5.1 (Cont.)

Title of enterprise	Date of sale	Basis of sale (assets or package of shares in %)	Firm-buyer	Debts payable (Tenge million)[a]	Debts receivable (Tenge, million)[e]	Investment (US$ million) million	Bonus (US$ million)	Value of agreement total[b]
1	2	3	4	5	6	7	8	9
AO Zheskaz-ganskii GOK	8.12.95 8.02.96	40	Novaresources SG 25	282.44	7 231	40	5.4	45.4
Karagandins-kaya TES 2	17.04.96	property complex	AO Ispat Karmet	597.313	359.641	36.5	0.92	42.53
AO Ermakovs-kaya GRES	02.05.96	property complex 53	Japan Chrome Corporation	2 166.07	1 203.88	258.2	1.51	259.71
Karaganda Shakhta Ugol	18.06.96	property complex	AO Ispat Karmet	11.3	7.5	100	82.34	194.99
Ekibastuskaya GRES 1	26.06.96	property complex	AES-Suntree Power Ltd.	3506	2 748.3	500	1.5	554.0
POEE Almaty Energo	31.07.96 17.09.96	property complex	Tractebel C.A.	8 696.9	6 653.86	300	7.31	358.43
Pavlodarskya TES 1	8.08.96	property complex	Whiteswan Ltd	1 177	1 434.7	11.6	1.04	113.72
Zheskazgans-kaya TES	8.08.96	property complex	Samsung	2 791	1 770.2	100	6.24	107.19

82

Table 5.1 *(Cont.)*

Title of enterprise	Date of sale	Basis of sale (assets or package of shares in %)	Firm-buyer	Debts payable (Tenge million)[a]	Debts receivable (Tenge, million)[e]	Investment (US$ million) million	Bonus (US$ million)	Value of agreement total[b]
1	2	3	4	5	6	7	8	9
Zambylskaya GRES	27.08.96	property complex	SP AO ZT VitolMunai	1 521.4	1 128.4	122	1.48	124.11
GAO Yuzhneftegas	28.08.96	89.5	Kharekein Kumkol Ltd	6 988.1	7 115.4	280	120	930.0[g]
AO Shimkent Nefteorgsintez	July 1996	94	Kazvitholding Ltd	1 313.2	1 648.2	150	60	230.0
AO Sary-Arka Pollimetall	19.09.96	39 51-IPF	Nakosta	441.2	327.9	21	1.2	28.6
Razrez Vostochnii + 34% property of Razrez Stepnoi	25.09.96	property complex	Japan Chrome Corp.	4 635.59	5 115.93	139.5	10.14	317.62[h]
Razrez Bogatyr +66% property of Razrez Stepnoi	18.10.96 complex	property	Access Industries, Inc.	6 258.05	7 498.03	550.0	40.0	801.2[i]
Razrez Severniy	18.10.96	property complex	AO Sverdlov energo	255.87	1 121.8	89.7	40.0	233.5[j]

Table 5.1 (*Cont.*)

Title of enterprise	Date of sale	Basis of sale (assets or package of shares in %)	Firm-buyer	Debts payable (Tenge million)[a]	Debts receivable (Tenge, million)[e]	Investment (US$ million) million	Bonus (US$ million)	Value of agreement total[b]
1	2	3	4	5	6	7	8	9
			RAO EES Rossii					
AO Lisakovskii GOK	24.10.96	51	AO Esil	703.83	720.23	23	7.5	46.04
Karagandinskaya GRES 2	October 1996	property complex	Independent Power Corp. PLC	1 209.22	245.11	400	1.1	418.81

[a] On the date of privatisation.
[b] The value of sale includes all the buyer liabilities (bonus, investment, debt repayment, wage arrears, budget arrears, non-budget arrears, royalty etc.)
[c] AO Ispart-Karmet – the value of the sale includes debts payable of Rehabilitation Bank (Tenge 2bn), debts repayment of US$50 m.
[d] Pavlodar Aluminium Plant – the value of the sale includes debts repayment of US$24.54m
[e] AO Ferrochrom – the value of the sale includes debts repayment of US$18.54m
[f] AO Sokolovo-Sarbaiskoe GOPO – the value of the sale includes debts repayment of US$19.84m
[g] Taking into consideration guaranteed payments to the budget of US$530m for 20 years
[h] Taking into consideration guaranteed payments to the budget of US$107.4m for 10 years
[i] Taking into consideration guaranteed payments to the budget of US$150m for 10 years
[j] Taking into consideration guaranteed payments to the budget of US$84.3m for 10 years

Source: Panorama, 1996, N 45.

Table 5.2 The progress of privatisation,[a] 1991–96

Title	1992		1993		Privatised 1994		1995		1996	
	Units	*As % of total*	*Units*	*As % of total*	*Units*	*As % of total*	*Units*	*As % of total*	*Units*	*As % of total*
Industry	211	5.1	422	15.7	543	8.8	48	1.5	437	10.8
Construction	110	2.7	237	8.8	313	5.0	52	1.7	45	1.1
Agriculture	918	22.1	344	12.8	628	10.1	514	16.4	138	3.4
Transport	180	4.3	469	17.4	90	1.5	28	0.9	101	2.5
Trade	1 201	29.0	392	14.6	1 834	29.6	1 358	43.2	1 519	37.5
Public catering	193	4.7	79	2.9	535	8.6	–	–	–	–
Consumer services	483	11.6	210	7.8	1 596	25.8	337	10.7	280	6.9
Municipal economy	104	2.5	46	1.7	195	3.1	–	–	–	–
Other branches	747	18.0	492	18.3	464	7.5	806	25.6	1 536	37.9
Total	4 147	100	2 691	100	6 198	100	3 143	100	4 056	100

[a] It must be noted that different sources such as *Kazak Economic Trends*, Mr Utepov (Chairman of Kazakstani State Committee of Privatisation) and the National Statistical Office provide different data regarding privatisation, which often contradict each other. The basis for this table is the data from the National Statistical Office.

Source: Operativnaya svodka gosudarstvennogo statisticheskogo komiteta, January 1997.

of the politics of privatisation in order for it to be successful than in the case in a society in which there is a clear distinction between economic and political decision-making.' (Schattschneider, 1960: 55).

According to Figure 5.1, privatisation as a national economic interest is formed through the points of view of the following groups: *government bureaucracy*, *corrupted officials* and *entrepreneurs*. Examination of the real situation in Kazakstan establishes that the passive role belongs to *farmers*, *peasantry*, *wage workers* and *office workers*. It is a mistake to argue that the ability of each group to represent their own interests are the same. To some extent this may be true for *government bureaucracy*, *corrupted officials* and *entrepreneurs*. *Owners* cannot satisfactorily express their interests, because this is a group which has yet to form.

Privatisation as a national economic interest is characterised by maximum limits for the use of personal rights on the share of state property by citizens; there are also limits for management enterprises which were privatised by Investment Privatisation Funds. These barriers were established by *government bureaucracy* and *corrupted officials*. Moreover, *government bureaucracy* and *corrupted officials* allege that they sought to reduce risk to the shareholders. This would be true if the enterprises were profitable and management will be suitable for the legal owners. In this case if the owner does not take part in the running of the enterprise there is a 100 per cent risk of bankruptcy and loss of property.

As a result, owners of estate property, financial resources and ideas cannot join their potential resources in one partnership and thus these commodities are not taken advantage of in order for them to be profitably used.

In this case even 'unfair' privatisation (through the enterprises being given away to their directors) would have been better for the economy rather than continuing the current policy of representing the present concept of privatisation as in the national economic interest.

The process of privatisation may have serious negative consequences. At present we are concerned with the fact that privatisation causes a reduction in output, because it leads to the breakdown of industrial links, regardless of their efficiency. Establishing new links will require a long period (due to the slowness of the process) and financial resources. But sometimes private owners change and re-change the nature of the final output in their enterprises. This will change the suppliers of intermediate products and consumers, dictate conditions for the delivery of goods and so on. In some cases enterprises are purchased for speculative resale, using fluctuations in both the rate of exchange and the growing monthly rate of inflation.

Privatisation can lead to increasing unemployment, and in the Kazakstani enterprises the numbers of workers, according to my estimation, exceeds the real needs of production by a factor of two. The official number of registered unemployed is 85 400 but in reality this figure is understated. There are a lot of plants and factories which do not work to their full capacity, working only for two or three days out of five, whilst their workers are registered to be in full-time employment. This is an example of hidden unemployment. According to independent sources, on 1 January 1995 there were 1200 enterprises and institutions employing 423 000 people, which had stopped production partially or fully (on 1 January 1994 these figures were lower – 597 enterprises employing 223 000 people respectively). In Kazakstan there are 160 000 people who are laid off temporarily, 70 per cent of these are unpaid. The level of hidden unemployment at the beginning of this year was 9.5 per cent of the economically active population.

Perhaps during the process of privatisation a contradiction can arise, between the necessity of participation in privatisation by foreign investors and the desire of home businessmen and in particular of managers of enterprises who would like to receive rights to a part of the former state property.

The likelihood of being without investment support due to the new owners' lack of financial resources to purchase enterprises and invest in production is one of the more dangerous consequences of privatised enterprises.

This model is flawed, because it contradicts the nature of the market economy insofar as it attempts to decrease the level of state ownership to 35–40 per cent. Such a decrease is unrealistic, and this could in turn cause the collapse of large parts of the national economy.

Currently estimating the effect from privatisation is difficult. The set of indicators could, for example, include:

1. The effect of the legislative process, the number of completed privatisations, the correlation between costs (to prepare enterprises for the privatisation process, payment of consultancy, advertisement etc.) and output (including sources received by the state budget). Besides this, in such a correlation we must take losses of the state budget into consideration, including enterprise debt writing off etc.
2. The effect of the period during which the enterprise is undergoing privatisation. This would include the speed of restructuring, labour productivity, whether privatisation helps in attracting investment, etc.

Most information regarding preparing enterprises for privatisation, preparation of auctions, costs of advertisement, has a confidential nature. In addition, most of the data upon which the above rely is not readily available, to either the Kazakstan National Statistical Office nor to potential investors. Accordingly, it is virtually impossible to produce a reliable estimation of the effects of privatisation.

It is, however, possible to remark that actual figure of state budget income from privatisation is different from that planned. Indeed, the real sale prices of approximately half of the sold enterprises were 50 per cent lower than that previously estimated.

It is realistic to withdraw state control in sectors serving the general population in retail areas, such as commerce and public catering. However, present government assets in capital intensive industries such as air, rail and other heavy industry should remain under state control. In certain industries, state control may be diluted to attract external investment through the establishment of joint ventures, or through permitting the establishment of competitors in the private sector.

Given the high level of state ownership of the means of agricultural production, mass privatisation and the disbanding of collective farms and state farms could lead to the collapse of agriculture, and turn the country from being one of the leading net exporters among agricultural exporters in the CIS to a major net importer of major food products.

By 1996, privatisation also embraced other sectors of the economy such as health and education.

The formation of a private sector before the year 2000 is very unlikely, except in trade and consumer service. Private enterprises in branches of industry can probably be formed in agriculture, the clothing industry, knitted-goods industry, tanning industry, boot and shoe industry and other sub-branches. These branches are on a small production scale with a low level of capital and a small amount of employees, and as a rule are family businesses.

The population does not have enough financial resources for the creation of new large and medium private enterprises. Therefore the formation of a large private sector in the Kazakstani economy has to move in an evolutionary way, gradually creating a layer of large entrepreneurs that can be privatised, expect those that are strategically valuable, whilst taking into account the interests of security, military and conservation of surroundings.

First, it is better to privatise unprofitable and inefficient enterprises, (accounting for nearly 30 per cent of all enterprises), because past experience in Kazakstan shows the negative consequences of doing the opposite (see above). This can then be followed, in stages, by privatisation of other enterprises in the creation of 'closed' enterprises (where ownership is restricted to employees). There has not, to date, been any major change in the profile of property ownership; and in fact because some enterprises have very unique valuable resources (e.g. equipment, human resources, unique process of production) the proceeds from the sale of 'closed' enterprises has resulted in only being ingested in changed figures in the national accounts. Accordingly, there has been no real inward capital investment in the enterprises concerned. Mass privatisation through the redistribution of the ownership of enterprises to the general public using a coupon system has been restricted to selected small enterprises, for example wholesale/retail outlets for the building materials industry. The proceeds from the sales remain in state hands, and the new owners of these privatised outlets do not generally have funds for further investment in developing their own manufacturing base. Accordingly, redistribution of property can give rise to reduced levels of production.

Effective economic structure assumes the existence of different forms of property, and their correlation is defined within certain concrete social-economic situations. During the first two phases of privatisation, the main criteria was the speed of privatisation, but not the formation of an effective economy. At present some preconditions exist for the transferring of privatisation on an economic base, where it is organised on a paying base. These are:

- stability of the social-political situation;
- understanding of the need for economic reforms;
- during the last few years a section of the population wishing to do business has formed;
- existence of available financial resources of population. According to an estimation by Narodnyi Bank, monetary savings are 2 billion Tenge (US$ 35 million) on 1 January 1995.

All these arguments would allow transfer to the phase of paying privatisation involving resources of physical and judicial bodies, including foreign investors.

It is necessary to connect privatisation with the process of technical reconstruction and the financial normalisation of enterprises, and also to involve the economic interests of future owners. In this case privatisation will have an economic base. The positive solution of this problem assumes considering the privatisation of every enterprise as part of a general business plan, that influences the choice of forms and methods of privatisation.

During the realisation of this, the main method of privatisation is competition between investment entrepreneurial projects (business plans). Their aim and essence of competition is the creation of enterprises on the basis of their reconstruction requirement. The main method of sale of enterprise, shares has to involve investment privatisation trusts, whose functions are:

- mobilisation of resources for restructuring and financial recovery;
- organising of management of the financial-investment process;
- consolidation of workers' shares and redemption of the enterprises' stock.

The business plan is the foundation of the creation, existence and appointment of the management of the trust. The government transfers its shares to trusts whilst remaining their owner during the carrying out of the business plan.

The government, through certain carriers of public authorities (State Property Committee, Ministry of Economy and so on), should found these trusts. The main difference in the described scheme of privatisation from the existing one is the fact that the buying of shares is made through the profits received from the current business plan, whereas beforehand the money for this would have come from wages or other personal sources of income.

As a consequence of employing this scheme the necessary economic conditions for positive effects of privatisation will be able to occur, such as:

- 20 per cent of the total volume of resources necessary for running the business plan will be free of all taxes;
- the trust will receive credit guaranteed by the government for the last of 80 per cent of volume of resources;
- in order to increase the volume of investment, enterprises have a right to issue privileged shares for sale;
- during the first two years the profits of the enterprises will not be taxed at all and will be taxed at a reduced rate for the following two years;
- the insurance payments payable in order to insure investments will be excluded from the taxable profit.

The evaluation of privatised property will use the following methods: inventory making, on the basis of the size of profit; on the basis of expected profits and profitability.

Thus the main aim of privatisation is to increase the effectiveness of the economy through creating effectively functioning projects based on private and mixed forms of ownership. There are three interrelated aims; attracting the necessary financial resources in order to increase government income, decreasing the amount of money spent on financing the public sector, and stabilisation and growth of the economy.

In spite of appearances, privatisation is not creating a system of economic measures which will allow the transformation of the Kazakstani economy to the market. This is not happening because privatisation is created through the expression of the interests of several groups. Frequent changes in *government bureaucracy* inevitably result in changing methods of privatisation.

The horrors resulting from attempts by groups to 'manage' privatisation, even to the point of assuming the role of citizens, who have the rights to state property within the economy, are not unique to Kazakstan; neither is the benefit that typically results from reducing these activities.

Owners of investment coupons cannot become owners of property at present, because coupons do not have a fixed value of property. Real owner's will appear later, when a security market has been created. The probability of a situation in which many owners of investment privatisation funds shares will influence management of companies is very small.

Free transfer of property in equal parts does not stimulate owners to feel like owners. A large part of the population are eager to have (for many reasons) a momentary return only, rather than to wait for an unspecified length of time for dividends. The activity of the *government bureaucracy* and directors of enterprises – the *nomenclaturnost* and the corruption of the process of privatisation gives people reasons not to believe in an opportunity of receiving dividends from shares.

Free transfer of property in equal parts is pure formal privatisation, which creates only formal owners (many of whom would get rid of personal investment coupons without any regrets).

The negative consequences after privatisation would occur not only because of lack of investment, but because there is not a legislative frame for post-privatisation enterprises. New owners of privatised property do not have a judicial responsibility and measures to act against them in case of breach of law simply do not exist.

The difficult situation in the economy is aggravated by privatisation of state property. The method of privatisation was not well thought out, and led to *prikhvatizaciya* (for personal purposes) enterprises by the *nomenklatura*, opportunists and local Mafia. It also led to uncertainty regarding the ownership of many of the enterprises, and as a result divided enterprises into their respective parts, etc. Consequently, these enterprises lost their production profile, and of course investment both by them and in them is most unlikely. The situation with newly privatised enterprises was so bad, the method of privatisation so wicked, that the question of post-privatisation support as a serious economic policy does not arise.

The most difficult and long-term consequence of the present privatisation is that property, resources and income have been redistributed without the creation of equal starting opportunities, whilst equal positions were created for most of the population. The gap between the very poor part of the population and the rich part of the population (whether or not this wealth has been obtained by legal means) is very wide indeed. This gap is now established and institutionalised, and is not likely to narrow, therefore it is difficult to obtain popular support for this governmental policy.

6 Structural Transformation

The Kazakstani government tried to put all economic reforms into order, and made some progress in the expression of its strategy. The 1996–98 Action Programme for the Deepening Reforms better covered all the dimensions of economic reforms.

The difficulties of industrial development for Kazakstan were exacerbated by the process of privatisation, the unattractiveness of investment, and difficulties with the adoption of a taxation code. The Kazakstani economy continues to suffer great difficulties, and will continue to do so until such problems as inter-enterprise arrears are satisfactorily resolved on both microeconomic and macroeconomic levels.

The shift of the economic structure to the material and energy consuming sources provide evidence of the difficulties inherent in out of date technological methodology being updated as a priority. It is impossible to consider the competitiveness until this has reached a successful conclusion.

1996–98 ACTION PROGRAMME FOR THE DEEPENING OF REFORMS

The government tried to carry out the 15 months' programme '*Programme of Government Activity in Increasing Reforms and Recovery from the Economic Crisis*' (1994). After the establishment of a strict monetary policy, stable exchange rate and decreasing of inflation by the National Bank of Kazakstan, the government reached a conclusion about accomplishment of economic recovery. They reasoned that the present anti-crisis programme was finished, and the question became how to create a new medium-term programme of economic reforms. The *1996–98 Action Programme for the Deepening of Reforms* was prepared by the Kazakstani government as a logical continuation of the previous programme.

The *1996–98 Action Programme for the Deepening of Reforms* begins with an economic analysis of the current situation, and the reader immediately learns that: 'from the middle of 1994 the first signs of macroeconomic stabilisation appeared in the economy …' (*1996–98 Action Programme for the Deepening of Reforms*, 1996: 4) It is strange (to say the least) to hear such things from governmental analysis, especially in a situation in which 'for seven months of the current year (1994) the inflation was 669.9 per cent ...' The style of presentation of the key results and the targets used throughout the programme gives the impression that this programme is not different to the previous five year-plans of the USSR. The statement 'one of the main social results of the reforms is that the taming of inflation substantially stopped the decreasing real income of the most lowest paid people with fixed incomes ...' (*1996–98 Action Programme for the Deepening of Reforms*, 1996: 5) is transparently farcical. When the delay with wages, pensions, and social payments has no limits, when the halt of inflation was only achieved through the means of decreasing the standard of living of these 'most lowest paid people with fixed incomes', such statements seem very cynical. By the time the reader reaches the second page of the programme it is possible to recognise who is 'guilty', and who will be 'guilty' in the near future in the event of unsuccessful economic reform. This is the micro level, where: feeling delay, that make consequence on the way of reform. Unclear sectoral economic policies, the absence of their coherent macro economic policy, amorphous measures in the sphere of enterprise reform lead to low results in the industrial sphere, which is expressed by a decline in production and an increase of arrears'. (*1996–98 Action Programme for the Deepening of Reforms*, 1996: 5). This is astonishing, because the main debtor is the state. But the impression left by this programme is that in Kazakstan there is a very good government, which has already finished all necessary global transformations and will now just polish some minor details. But in the event of something going wrong, the programme has already set the ground for a 'scapegoat' – the micro level.

The main aim of this programme is 'the securing of the results achieved in 1994–1995 in the area of stabilisation and structural-institutional transformations, stopping the decline in production, and afterwards providing an increase in the economy, and growth in the standard of living of the population' (*1996–98 Action Programme for the Deepening of Reforms*, 1996: 5). One of the main tasks for the government is a plan to decrease inflation from 26–28 per cent in 1996 to 9–12 per cent in 1998.

The programme is divided into six parts:

- Macro economic stabilisation;
- Structural-institutional transformations;
- Development of important sectors of the economy;
- Social policy;
- Management of the economy; and
- Special parts

Macro economic stabilisation: this covers the main activities in monetary and credit policies, budget policy, and external borrowing, taking into consideration the debts of the state, improving trade balance and balance of payments.

Structural-institutional transformations: the most important problem here is reform of the financial system of the state, transformation of the forms of property, enterprises reforms, and development of entrepreneurship, land reform and so on.

Development of important sectors of the economy: this part concerns the restructuring of the main sectors of the economy.

Social policy: is connected with the solution of such problems as increasing financial assistance and increasing social protection of the population with a low standard of living.

Management of the economy: explains how the different parts of the economy are supposed to be connected.

Special parts: Consists of improvement of law and order, the battle with economic crime and corruption, as well as the problems of providing an adequate legislative base for reforms.[1]

The weakest aspect of the programme is the plan for the liquidation of the debts crisis. The government obviously does not have a clear idea about the method to solve this problem, and simply forgot about its own debts (wages arrears – state enterprises, pensions, etc).

The programme certainly has more logic than previous programmes. Every sector of the economy has evidently found a place in the programme, links are established between the parts of programme, and there are much more coherent plans of reform.

INDUSTRIAL AND INVESTMENT POLICY

Industrial strategy cannot be considered in the abstract; it must be located within the context of overall economic strategy. The challenge of industrial restructuring confronts enterprises in all sectors and in all countries as they face increasing global competition, new technologies, and new forms of production organisation. But the challenges facing Kazakstani enterprises are greater than most. This is partly because the competition in the Soviet Union was of such a nature that it led firms away from the factors which now dominate world markets, such as product innovation, quality and speed of response. In the internal division of labour in the USSR, Kazakstan played the role of a producer of raw materials, and therefore the legacy is only relatively developed sectors of the economy.

This has resulted in an industrial structure in which key parts of the value chain (not only design, but also marketing) were located in other Republics, and one in which the transfer of components along the value-chain occurred on a non-price oriented basis; inter-enterprise links often involved complicated and long-term relationships which are now proving difficult to unravel. Confronted by this wide range of severe obstacles to industrial development, it is clear that there is a large number of 'big issues' confronting both economic and industrial policy in Kazakstan. It is essential that industrial strategy be carefully focused. It is also critical that the macroeconomic strategy be appropriately oriented to complement the industrial strategy which is adopted.

The difficulties which were created by raising of the inter-enterprise arrears, influenced the enterprise's preferences in current consumption of causes (I will discuss this later).

It would thus appear that there is a difference in approach between the economic and industrial strategies currently being pursued in Kazakstan. Whilst the economic strategy is largely concerned with the establishment of a broad market environment, the industrial strategy is more specifically focused on detailed policy instruments, and is more 'interventionist' in its approach to the industrial sector.

The question is whether these sets of policies will be effective in promoting appropriate industrial restructuring of Kazakstan's economy. Despite the fact that these policies do confront some of the weaknesses of past policies (for instance, providing more autonomy to enterprise management and aligning prices more closely to economic costs and benefits) there are important areas in which this policy trajectory is not an adequate response to the new challenges which have to be confronted. The central problem is that there is a variety of different types of market economies, each with particular trajectories. The structural policy has to be elaborated widely, having included structural changes of the forms of property.

The decline in output has been constant since 1991. Figure 6.1 shows that in 1995 industrial output was 46 per cent of 1990 industrial output.

The distortion of prices might give the reader a wrong picture, because technically we can see the increasing share in production of heavy industry from 1980 to 1995. When *Perestroika* started, the discussions about the disproportionate weight of the industrial structure began. As a result of years of reforms, sectors of the economy which were related to scientific-technical progress (such as chemical, oil chemical, food, light industries) began to disappear (Figure 6.2) and the industrial structure became worse. Under import competition a lot of industries were disadvantaged. If such a situation continues, only heavy industry will exist in Kazakstan, which will have a negative influence on the ecology in the country, which remains in difficulties.

In economic sectors such as electricity, fuels and metallurgy (basically in the raw material sectors) the situation has stabilised. After 1994 production output (in average terms) was 60–64 per cent of the 1990 level. In addition, in 1996, exploration of oil and gas achieved 90 per cent of the 1990 level (Table 6.1).

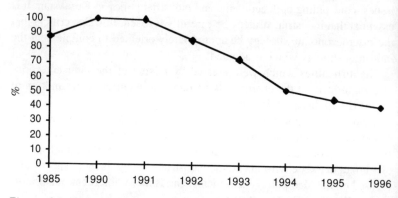

Figure 6.1 Industrial output (percentage change in output, 1990 = 100%) (*Source*: Figure was drawn based on data from *Statisticheskii Yezhegodnik Kazakhstana, 1991, 1993, 1995, 1996, 1997*)

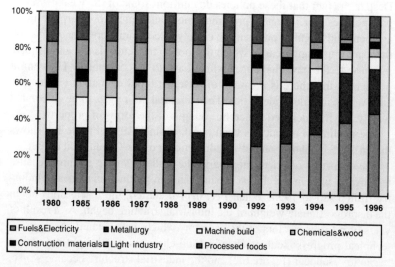

Figure 6.2 Structure of industrial production, 1980–96 (%) (*Source*: Figure was drawn based on data from *Statisticheskii Yezhegodnik Kazakhstana, 1991, 1993, 1995*)

Table 6.1 Energy, raw material products, primary manufactured products, 1980–96

Indicator	1980	1985	1988	1989	1990	1991	1992	1993	1994	1995	1996
Electricity, 10^6 kwh	61 530	81 263	88 417	89 657	87 379	85 984	82 700	77 444	66 397	66 659	58 657
Oil, 10^3 tonnes	18 656	22 839	25 516	25 388	25 820	26 591	25 848	22 975	20 279	20 450	23 000
Natural gas, 10^6 cub. m	4 314	5 456	7 134	6 710	7 114	7 885	8 113	6 685	4 488	5 916	6 396
Coal, 10^6 tonnes	115	131	143	138	131	130	127	112	105	83	77
Iron ore, 10^3 tonnes	25 763	22 977	24 342	23 764	23 846	21 993	17 671	13 129	10 521	14 902	13 174
Chromite ore, 10^3 tonnes	3 300	3 259	3 508	3 571	3 660	3 616	3 452	2 968	2 103	2 417	1 103
Crude steel, 10^3 tonnes	5 967	6 155	6 766	6 831	6 754	6 377	6 063	4 558	2 969	3 027	3 216
Rolled metal, 10^3 tonnes	4 403	4 448	4 874	5 013	4 955	4 721	4 426	3 489	2 357	2 153	2 399

Source: Statisticheskii ezhegodnik Kazakhstana, 1991, 1995, 1996, 1997.

At the same time the situation was worse in the following sectors of the economy: textiles, clothing, building materials, shoes, machine building, wood products (in other words, the industries of final production) – see Table 6.2). In 1996 the average output of these sectors was 8 per cent of 1990 and the conclusion that these industries had collapsed in inescapable.

There exists a huge crisis in technology, as the total volume of industrial production decreased by 200 per cent compared with 1990, but at the same time that electro-energy production decreased only by 24 per cent, electro-energy consumption was decreased only by 10–15 per cent. This demonstrates that electro-capacity has increased, which means in technical terms that the equipment is old.

The current problems of industrial sectors in Kazakstan are as follows:

- small and medium enterprises, particularly those of a start-up nature, generally experience a range of difficulties in relation to obtaining finance, marketing expertise, quality procedures, and so on;
- changes in work organisation, in the structure of management and in inter-firm relations require profound alterations to social relations; experience shows that the changes diffuse at a slow pace when left to market pressure alone;
- human resources lie at the core of industrial competence. For a variety of reasons, enterprises tend to under invest in industrial training and do little to promote appropriate forms of education;

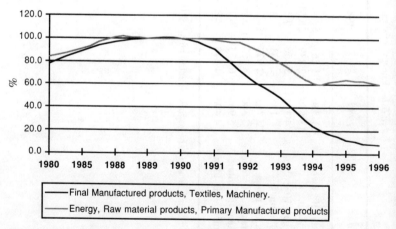

Figure 6.3 Output of production (in average terms) in some industrial sectors (1990 = 100%) (*Source*: Tables 6.1 and 6.2)

Table 6.2   Final manufactured products, textiles, machinery, 1980–96

Indicator	1980	1985	1988	1989	1990	1991	1992	1993	1994	1995	1996
Fabrics, 10^6 sq. m	178	289.2	324	330	325.5	230	228.4	188.1	107.1	31.1	28
Knitted wear, 10^6 units	95.6	100.3	108.1	122.9	126.9	111.6	690	50.2	29.1	8.5	3.1
Socks and tights, 10^6 pairs	69.0	76.7	80.5	82.6	87.7	83.1	74.4	71.5	41.0	11.5	5.6
Shoes, 10^6 pairs	34.2	36.9	38.6	39.3	40.5	37.9	24.5	16	7.7	2.1	1.4
China, 10^3 units	9 280	26 912	38 307	36 749	34 276	33 604	32 934	32 463	17 288	9 870	5 302
Washing machines, 10^3 units	175.2	183.3	166.2	265	367.4	391.1	370	255	88	46	23.2
Metal cutting lathes, units	3 017	2 848	2 214	2 307	2 578	2 381	1 629	1 193	429	57	126
Forge-press machinery, units	1 439	1 295	1 161	1 205	1 173	1 165	757	730	434	269	110
Excavators, units	1 803	1 877	570	528	710	618	312	210	32	0	11
Bulldozers, units	8 863	13 670	14 810	15 308	13 328	10 288	3 494	4 234	695	521	246
Mineral fertilisers, 10^3 tonnes	1 262	1 430	1 737	1 704	1 656	1 516	880	304	126	197	191
Timber, 10^3 cub m	2 183	2 313	2 403	2 512	2 337	1 974	1 664	1 170	979	883	653
Cardboard, 10^3 tonnes	108.3	132	163	158	156	124.3	81	43	16	8	7.4
Paper, tonnes	17 600	10 797	2 700	2 900	1 510	1 029	700	2 108	721	174	67
Chairs, 10^3 units	860	988	1 247	1 268	1 014	819	531	260	56	45	–*
Bricks (conventional size) 10^6 units	2 983	3 079	3 866	3 902	3 674	3 350	3 346	2 261	1 088	583	283
Pre-fabricated ferro-concrete structures and parts, 10^3 cub m	6 067	6 575	7 746	7 717	7 504	7 221	5 450	3 604	1 511	831	491

* Figures not available

Source: Statisticheskii ezhegodnik Kazakhstana, 1991, 1995, 1996, 1997.

- knowledge of external markets tends to be low at the enterprise level. Thus, particularly in the case of small and medium enterprises, there is a tendency to focus on the domestic market.

These problems take place in all economies and most of the more successful economies have taken steps to correct these imperfections in the functioning of markets. The problem here is in the danger of non-comprehension of these features for Kazakstan, or understanding only at the level of rhetoric, as opposed to knowing what to do about it. At the present time the Statistical Office of the Government of Kazakstan has tried to convince everybody that the process of macro-stabilisation is taking place (Box 6.1) and GDP is growing.

Box 6.1   The Kazakstani 'method' of GDP calculation

The recent official data of GDP dynamics gives reasons to distrust the picture of economic recovery which the Government of Kazakstan has tried to present. The first argument is simple enough. During 1995 the figures for the GDP of 1994 was changed at least three times. The first estimation did not suit, because the increase in the decline in production in 1994 was very high – 30 per cent. Then the volume of GDP was increased to 464 billion Tenge, which allowed for the growth of GDP decline to be 25.4 per cent. The last time it was declined to 449 billion Tenge, so the change in the decline of GDP in 1995 was lower than the politically projected level of 10 per cent. The official version of such calculations was that these calculations did not take into account various factors. But in such a situation it would be necessary to start the re-calculation from 1991 – the base year for estimation of reforms. In this instance we will lose the ability to exercise continuity of analysis, and it is obvious that such indicators would be unable to adequately characterise the dynamic of the economic development.

The 'new' indicator of *households* – which was recently introduced to the Kazakstani national statistics by National Statistical Office is problematic.

The first point which is unclear is how the sector *households* was defined. The definition of *households* is the set of five industrial sectors of the economy:

Timber and woodworking industry
Construction material industry

Light industry
Food industry
Flour-grinding – cereals and mixed fodder industry

Sources indicate that 2000 households are used for the monthly calculation of this industrial data. With the whole of the Kazakstani economy remaining in crisis, the use of a sample 2000 appears particularly subjective. In all industrial indicators there is a high decline in production in 1996 in comparison to 1995:

Timber and woodworking industry	–22.5 per cent
Construction material industry	–32.7 per cent
Light industry	–17.7 per cent
Food industry	–27.1 per cent
Flour-grinding – cereals and mixed fodder industry	–17.2 per cent

If the figures for household production are included, the same sectors portray a very different picture:

Timber and woodworking industry	+7.0 per cent
Construction material industry	–31.8 per cent
Light industry	+14.5 per cent
Food industry	+32.7 per cent
Flour-grinding – cereals and mixed fodder industry	–9.5 per cent

The question which might arise is who has consumed the production of the household sector, the volume of which has made such a demonstrable difference. Whilst the production sphere is in crisis, consumption is in an even worse position. The production of foodstuff (meat, sausages, milk, butter, flavour) decreased by 2 per cent – 39 per cent, non-foodstuff production (refrigerators – 50 per cent, dishes-china – 46 per cent, shoes – 30 per cent) and light industry production (jersey – 63 per cent) also remain in crisis. At the same time the figure of retail turnover in 1996 (in relative prices with 1995) is 202.5 billion. Tenge (or in other words there is an increase of 138.5 per cent). For registered trade enterprises the same figure is 114.9 billion Tenge (or 57 per cent of total amount), an increase 103.8 per cent. The rest of the amount comes from goods and foods markets, here the increase was 247 per cent. But according to the official information of the Kazakstani statistical office 'assortment of goods

Box 6.1 Continued

which are offering to consumer represent generally by import goods' (Nasionalno-Statesticheskoe Agenstvo Respubliki Kazakhstan, 1997: 64). The figure for import goods increased in 1996 only by 13.9 per cent (Tenge 36 billion) in comparison to 1995. According to the Kazakstani Statistical Office, goods turnover on the open markets was increased by Tenge 65 billion. But it is obvious that not all shares of import, which were increased were sold on the open market.

The obvious question is what in this case the population is selling on the open markets, where increase is 247 per cent, at the same time as other types of retail trade are increasing only on 103.8 per cent. Another point which is confusing is: on the open markets the goods are bought by the population and the point that the population is buying something means that population has available money for this, but from which source? '... the main source of monetary income of population is wage ...' (Nationalno-Statesticheskoe Agenstvo Respubliki Kazakhstan, 1997: 71). In 1996 the average per capita income increased by 5.6 per cent. At the same time, the consumer price index increased by 28.7 per cent. The real average wage increased by 3.5 per cent, but according to the *Kazakstan Economic Trends* (January, 1997) the real wage was decreased by 2 per cent in 1996 compared with 1995. Taking into consideration that the share of industry and trade in GDP is 21.3 per cent and 17.1 per cent respectively, we can try to calculate the real changes in GDP by 1996. During the last two years the decline in industry (without households) monthly is 0.85 per cent. Therefore it is impossible to speak about growth in industry in 1996 by 0.3 per cent, but it is possible to conclude that Industry decreased by 9.9 per cent which decreases GDP immediately by 2 per cent. According to the Kazakstani Statistical Office by 1996 on the open markets production was sold on Tenge 108 billion. (or in comparative prices in 2.5 times higher than in 1995). In this case the share of open markets is 7.6 per cent of GDP, but if we take into consideration the fact that we cannot find spare money (63 per cent of population income is spent on food), which the population can spend, and assuming that the total amount of production would be the same in 1996 as in 1995, GDP is therefore decreased by 4 per cent.

For the most part, the average wage remained in arrears (which accounted for over 21 per cent of the total wage bill, not including pensions and subsidies). The paradoxical situation is that demand is decreasing, the production of the household sector is increasing, and at the same time very actively consuming when the market is full of a lot of import goods.

It is not correct to use the indicator *households* for calculation of GDP at the present moment. The production of households is connected only with personal consumption. Therefore it is possible to confirm that the economic decline in Kazakstan is continuing; according to the estimations of the Centre for Euro-Asian Studies (the University of Reading, UK) GDP did not increase by 1.1 per cent, but decreased by 4–6 per cent compared with 1995.

During the years of economic transformation structural changes took place in the Kazakstani GDP. So, in 1996 industry accounted for only 21.3 per cent of GDP, down from over 28 per cent in 1992. This situation could be explained partially because the trade arms of industrial companies are now counted as trade (before they belonged to the industrial sector). Construction's share in GDP has fallen because of the withdrawal of government subsidies and is only 3.6 per cent. The share of agriculture in GDP was falling from 20.8 per cent in 1992 to 12.8 per cent in 1996. But the share of services is growing very rapidly, with trade the second largest generator of GDP, accounting for more than 17.1 per cent (*Kazakstan Economic Trends*, January 1997: Table 3.2). All these changes could be characterised possibly as positives, which would be moving the Kazakstani economic structure towards the economic structure of the developed countries, if they were not coinciding with overall economic decline.

In the conditions of the transitional economy the economic development is characterised by serious structural changes, but the methods of estimating these structural changes are not adequate to the economic reality. As a result aggregate indicators of economic growth have a very strong dependence upon methods of calculations which were adopted as appropriate methods for transitional economies. In reality they were borrowed from the experience of countries with more or less stable economies. So, with the different speed of industrial decline in the different industrial sectors, with various reasons for cutting production, dynamic changes of prices on the same groups of goods and services, it is impossible to analyse the structural changes in the economy. Taking into consideration the difference in the growth of prices on industrial and agricultural production, payable services and transport service, it is very difficult to characterise value changes in GDP as progressive. In addition, agriculture in the real economy will continue to occupy an important place.

Box 6.1   Continued

The most difficult consequence of such estimation of GDP is that on the basis of non-realistic data it is possible to take a number of mistaken measures for improving of the economic situation, it would allow the process of destroying sectors of the economy to continue, which is of course dangerous for national economic security. At the present time macroeconomic indicators are presented in a way designed to indicate economic recovery. If this was taken seriously, it would lead to increased credits for the economy. In reality of course, there is a lack of macroeconomics stability, the consequences of which might potentially be growing inflation and such credit sources could be wasted with huge losses.

The stabilisation of the industrial sphere is occurring only through the growth of export production with nearly the whole satisfaction of demand by imports. This could be characterised as *producing products which are not consumed and consuming products which are not produced*. It is necessary to remark that if by 1995 fuel, metallurgical, chemical and oil chemical industries increased the growth of exports, by 1996 only fuel and metallurgical industries provided the growth. Stabilisation in the industrial field is being achieved only by the three sectors: fuel industry (growth of 5.6 per cent), non-ferrous metallurgy (growth of 10.5 per cent), and the printing industry (growth of 26.7 per cent). The share of the polygraph industry in the total volume of industrial production is only 0.3 per cent. In all other industries the decline in production continues, ranging from 4.1 per cent in electro-energy to 39.8 per cent in the microbiological industry.

The situation in the industry today is defined completely by the activity of the foreign firms, which are owners of enterprises of the export sector of the Kazakstani economy – fuel industry and metallurgy.[2] In industry only the volume of export production is on the increase. The main products of this industry are semi-finished products of the fuel industry and metallurgy, whilst at the same time the production of the ferrous metals is decreasing. Other products such as ferroalloy, chrome products, etc., decreased as well. All these products were formerly exported to the CIS countries, and at present 80 per cent of export production is to non-CIS countries, therefore ferrous metallurgy has become a non-profitable sector of the Kazakstani economy. The manufacturing sector (which includes machine-building) remains in crisis as well.

The market in Kazakhstan *sic* is too narrow; many manufactured goods simply do not correspond to the demands of local users. Thus, because of the depressed condition of the machine-building, chemical, and petrochemical industries, Kazakhstan is undergoing a gradual deindustrialisation of its economy – a process of economic regression fraught with major, long-term consequences. (Rumer, 1996: 206).

The share of industry in GDP has continued to shrink since 1993 (Figure 6.4). One of the reasons for this decline of all industrial enterprises was a lack of financial resources.

In the earlier stage of transition the share of resources available to state enterprises was not enough to halt the reduction in investment activity. The reduction in investment activity (Figure 6.5) was dominated by the decline of investment in the state sector of the economy, but the share of investment in the state sector of economy in relation to the total volume of investment was a dominant 67.0 per cent.

One of the main reasons for the crisis in the investment sphere is that privatisation is not supported by adequate activity in the distribution of investment resources, and therefore does not affect the property sphere. In spite of appearances privatisation is not creating a system of economic measures which will transform Kazakhstan's economy to a market system (Kalyuzhnova, 1995/96b 17). The very complicated development of privatisation, and imperfections in the stock market make it difficult to evaluate their influence on the general situation of investment activity. The

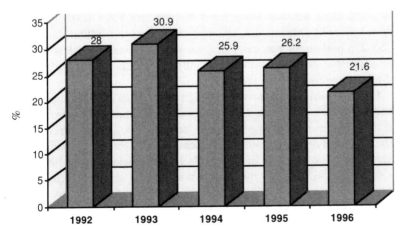

Figure 6.4 The share of industry in GDP, 1992–96 (*Source*: *Statistichevskii Yezhegodnik Kazakhstana, 1991, 1993, 1995, 1997*)

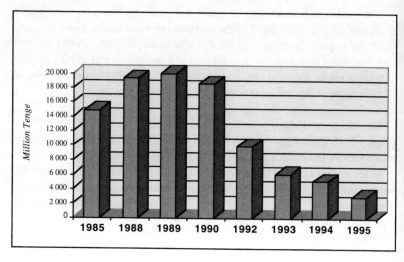

Figure 6.5 Capital investment (in constant 1991 prices) (*Source*: *Statistichevskii Yezhegodnik Kazakhstana, 1991, 1993, 1995, 1996*)

changes in trade of stock values which took place in 1992–93 did not drive the capital market to become a whole system. The infrastructure of the market was underdeveloped, securities and capital markets had not yet been formed. The speed of inflation loss in the value of the populations savings was higher than its nominal increase.

In times of economic recession, foreign investment is very important for support of national investment activity. By 1995 Kazakstan had signed a credit agreement to the amount of US$ 1.1 billion, including US$ 236 million for purchases of consumer goods and US$ 864 million for industrial goods. However, the influence of foreign capital on the republic investment market remains small.

The main difficulty in attracting foreign credits is an imperfect legislative base, and a lack of mechanism of choice and realisation of investment projects, as well as rent-seeking behaviour, corruption and other disincentives. The Law on Foreign Investments, which regulates foreign investments in Kazakstan came into force in 1995, replacing the previous law of 1991. The government tried to attract foreign investors into the industrial sector of the Kazakstani economy, but bureaucracy is a major problem for any project which lacks clear and influential high-level political backing. Foreign companies which have leased Kazakstani enterprises often have a difficult time.

The history of the lease of the Karaganda Metallurgical Combine[3] (*Karmetkombinat*) to a foreign firm can be included in the list of negative examples of transitional governments. In the initial attempt to lease *Karmetkombinat*, West-Alpine and the USX-US Steel Group were involved, and the government had great difficulty handling the delicate situation. After extended debates and complaints from foreign firms about the mishandling of the *Karmetkombinat* situation, the Kazakstani government sold the enterprise to Ispat International (a UK-based firm) in November 1995.

The incompetent behaviour of the government bureaucracy was demonstrated in the attempts to sell off the Vasilkovskoe mine. Foreign mining companies had been interested in the mine since 1992 and the Kazakstani authority's seemingly incompetent behaviour has served to erode investor confidence. The mine is one of the world's largest, reportedly containing around 7.7 million ounces of gold. In June 1996 the government awarded the mine to a consortium led by the Teck Corporation of Canada, following an open tender. Teck's partners were Bakyrchik Gold, which had been developing a gold mine in eastern Kazakstan since 1993 and is listed on the London Stock Exchange, and First Dynasty Mines Ltd (listed in Toronto). The Teck-led consortium will in theory acquire 80 per cent of the equity in a joint venture with Kazakstan, at a price of $85 million. The consortium will plough a further $360 million into the mine and will operate it for 25 years. The losers in the tender were the state-owned mining company, Altyn-Almas, Dundee Bancorp (Canada), Cogema (France) and Lonrho Mining (UK). A number of large mining firms boycotted the tender. The key player in the new deal was Robert Friedland, a Singapore-based mining tycoon. However, mismanagement by the Kazakstani authorities soon ensured that the deal ran into trouble. First, the deadline for the end of negotiations was extended from 1 July to 11 August 1996. Of the $85 million, $35 million was expected to be returned by Kazakstan to Placer Dome of Canada. The latter was awarded the mine in 1995 amid considerable controversy. The European Bank for Reconstruction and Development refused to finance the project and the country's reputation was tarnished. The Kazakstani authorities wanted to repay Placer Dome its $35 million deposit out of the money to be paid by Teck, which reportedly offered to repay Placer Dome directly – an offer rebuffed by Kazakstan, which then failed to repay the deposit, as scheduled on 4 July 1996. The second deadline, for the end of negotiations, was missed and Kazakstan reportedly then offered the mine to Lonrho. The British firm responded by saying that it would not rush to make an offer. Then in September 1996, Bakyrchik pulled out of the Teck-led consortium and gave up its share to First Dynasty Mines. By January 1997 the bid from Teck Corporation was rejected and the mine is still without an investor, three years after the first tender.

The 'marriage' between *Kazaktelekom* and Deutsche Telecom was destroyed in January 1997. The German telecom munication giant was asking for a monopoly on telecommunication services to protect the potential revenue stream. At the present time *Kaztelekom* has debts of Tenge 11.3 billion and DM460 million owed to Germany that would have been cleared by the Deutsche Telecom deal. The original negotiations were that Deutsche Telecom would obtain DM825 million worth of shares in *Kaztelekom*, or 49 per cent of the equity, in part through a debt-for-equity swap. Kazakstan could owe DM460 million to Kreditanstalt fur Wiederaufbau of Germany. Deutsche Telecom was going to invest DM170 million and to pay DM120 million to the Kazakstani government.

At the present time the Kazakstani government is looking to sell 40 per cent of *Kaztelekom* to a strategic investor who is willing to assume responsibility for the debts of *Kaztelekom*, and also replace 500 000 old lines and commit to providing 3 million lines within 5 years, culminating in 4.2–4.5 million lines within 10 years.

In December 1996 the Bakyrchik Mining Joint Venture (BMJV), which was a 40: 60 joint venture between Bakyrchik Gold and the Kazakstani government, was restructured, with Kazakstan selling Bakyrchik Gold its share. This meant that BMJV became a fully foreign-owned venture. In return for a one-year working capital loan of $20 million and part of the cost of buying out the Kazakstani government Indochina Goldfields (Singapore) bought the remaining 15 per cent of the Kazakstani government's former stake from Bakyrchik Gold, which means Bakyrchik Gold's stake has now increased from 40 per cent to 85 per cent. The cost of the Kazakstani government's 60 per cent stake in BMJV was $65 million. Indochina Goldfields owns 26.6 per cent of Bakyrchik Gold, with the key player in both again being Robert Friedland. Bakyrchik expects to be producing gold by 1999 at a cost of $200 per oz, but only after making a further $220 million investment in the venture. Extraction rates could hit 1 million tons of ore containing 230 000 oz gold; total ore reserves are estimated at 13 million oz. Bakyrchik Gold was floated in 1993 on the London Stock Exchange.

The case of Phillip Morris involved more than a hundred decrees and decisions. After buying Almaty Tobacco Company in 1993, it signed an exclusive distribution deal with *Bakalaytorg*, which was the largest single distribution agency in Kazakstan.

During the Soviet Union period, *Bakalaytorg* was state owned, and largely output driven, which means it was not responsive to demand. The distribution deal with Almaty Tobacco Company (ATC) was for distribution of 14 billion 'sticks' a year, but failed to the extent that the first year saw distribution of only 200 million. The problem was in payment, as

Bakalaytorg insisted upon a consignment payment, but could provide no bank guarantees. The end result was a huge inventory backlog for the ATC, and Philip Morris closed the ATC for three months in mid-1994.

After spending a not inconsequential time searching for local distribution options, ATC eventually decided to use Cinava, a Monaco-based chain which had previously distributed Philip Morris products in the Ukraine. This arrangement in time (one and a half years) also failed, mainly because of subcontractor and pilferage problems.

The end result, after two and a half years of distribution problems, is that ATC has contracts with over 12 local distribution firms, accepts guarantees from the local Kazkommertz Bank, and has established a forward warehouse in Karaganda.

It is possible to conclude that the transfer of enterprises with future sale of their property still did not lead to a significant growth of investments. The main share of these investments is used for paying enterprise debts and increasing an enterprise's circulating capital. The interest of foreign investors is mainly concerned with ferrous and non-ferrous industries, and oil and gas, which means foreign investment is concentrating only upon the mining industries. Foreign investors who are putting in capital now are expecting to return a profit after 3–5 years, in order to cover the initial costs. Generally, foreign investors will receive their share of profit as a finished production of enterprises such as oil, finished metallurgical products, non-ferrous metals, and so on, which are the main items of Kazakstani exports. Therefore, from 1998 dividends of foreign investors will be a valuable part of Kazakstani exports, which means that the nominal growth of exports would not be accompanied by the growth of currency for these exports, and this of course would have a pronounced negative influence upon the balance of payments. Foreign investment in metallurgy in 1995 was 50.3 per cent of total foreign investment in Kazakstan, in oil and gas it was 34.7 per cent of total foreign investment in Kazakstan, and in the first quarter of 1996 the share of foreign investment to these sectors was 64.2 per cent and 33.7 per cent respectively. The main investors in the oil and gas industries are USA, France, Turkey, UK, Italy, Norway and Germany; in metallurgy they are South Korea, UK, Japan and Canada.

Recently the Kazakstani government transferred control of a lot of enterprises, which belong to the export sector of the economy to foreign companies. The official explanation of this is that the government tried to solve the debt problems, raise finance to pay overdue wages, pensions, and other payments to the population. 'This policy, unprecedented in world practice, threatens to wreak enormous harm to national economic interests: foreign firms that control such enterprises engage in a highly intensive export of raw materials to destinations outside the republic, sometimes at dumping prices...' (Rumer, 1996: 224).

All foreign investors have concerns: political and economic stability; laws and regulations; a relatively small domestic market; a high rate of obsolescence and depreciation of fixed capital, high production costs, and a large proportion of enterprises (especially in the manufacturing sector) that are not competitive or have little demand for their products; a negative balance of payments. The government's ambitious plan to move the capital from Almaty to Akmola (Central Kazakstan), where infrastructure is rudimentary, has discouraged some potential foreign investors as well.

Thirty per cent of all foreign investments are foreign direct investments (FDI). In 1995 the inflow of FDI was roughly $860 million, which is about 5 per cent of GDP. Kazakstan has put special emphasis on investment policies in its *1996–98 Action Programme for the Deepening of Reforms* and in its *Law about State Support of Direct Investment* (28 February 1997), through which it hopes to develop efficient and competitive industries. To implement the structural transformations Kazakstan needs 500 to 600 million dollars of foreign investments every year.

At the present time the foreign capital attracted to Kazakstan is in the form of credits, which now account for 77.6 per cent of total foreign capital. 'Of the 681.1 million dollars obtained as credits during the reform period, 42.4 per cent was invested in transportation and communication, 14.1 per cent in agriculture, and only 12 per cent in industry.' (Rumer, 1996: 218).

Economic growth and FDI inflows are closely related. The progress in attracting FDI in Kazakstan might come only through real economic recovery, a respect for international ethical standards, and an astute awareness and rational behaviour on the part of the government bureaucracy as well as a systematic economic policy.

THE NEW TAX CODE

The Tax Code signed by President Nazarbayev on the 24 April 1995 entered into force on 1 July 1995. The new tax code in Kazakstan provides for the following central government taxes: business income tax of 30 per cent, except for income derived from land, for which the rate is 10 per cent, individual income tax at progressive marginal rates from 5 per cent to 40 per cent; value-added tax of 20 per cent. There is a uniform business income tax of 30 per cent irrespective of the size of business. This is unfortunate. It would make sense for a rate for small business to be introduced (up to a certain level of taxable profit) to encourage the formation of those businesses. There are five national and six local taxes (see Table 6.3).

Table 6.3   Taxes in Kazakstan

Tax	Payer	Base	Rate
National taxes			
Income Tax	Resident companies Permanent Establishments of non-residents	Western-style business profits and capital gains dividends or net branch profit	30% 15% withholding
	Other non-residents	Certain payments received from Kazak entities or PEs	5%–20%
	Individuals	Income from business Income from employment including 'benefits in kind'	Up to 40% Up to 40%
VAT	Business	Outputs minus inputs, 'EEC style'	Monthly 20% Export zero-rated Finance (exempt and land)
Excises	Legal and physical persons	Luxury goods (Article 76)	To be set by Cabinet of Ministers
Securities Tax	Issues/sellers of securities	Value of securities (Article 88)	Article 89
Mineral Resources	Mineral resource users	Super profits, royalties, bonuses	Article 94–104
Local taxes			
Asset Tax	Asset owners	Business capital assets	5% of value
Land tax	Land users	Land quality	Per Articles 108, 112, 114
Vehicle Tax	Vehicle owners	Vehicle power	Table in Article 128
Business Registration fee Activities licence fee Auction Tax	To be determined by the Cabinet Ministers		

Source: Table was composed on the basis of the Republic of Kazakstan Tax Code.

For most businesses investing in Kazakstan, the key economic taxes were Income Tax for companies and individuals, and VAT.

Exports are reassessed at a zero rate which acts as a credit for input taxes. Excise duty is to be charged on a set of specified imported and domestically produced goods: a 0.5 per cent tax on the nominal value of all securities issued including stocks and bonds, and a 0.3 per cent tax on the selling price of secondary sales of securities are to be charged. There is also a tax on bonuses, royalties, and excess profits on the users of mineral resources; and an annual land tax, property tax, and vehicle registration fee. Going from 48 taxes and fees to 11 types of taxes will no doubt contribute greatly toward the country's economic stabilisation. Reforms include the elimination of over 30 taxes and special fund contributions. It is not clear whether capital gains tax is applied to individuals who hold shares in companies.

There is a withholding dividend tax remitted from Kazakstani companies or branches which does not deal with any profit, interest etc. remitted from other countries in the region to Kazakstan and then remitted onward to countries outside the region.

Foreign investors hold up Kazakstan's new tax code as a good pattern for other countries. There appears to be an Anglo-American style of drafting and content (e.g. Article 41 which reflects an Anglo-America tax treatment of long-term contracts). This code should provide some alleviation to multinationals that have business in the oil-rich regions of Kazakstan. Among other benefits, it will allow them to deduct production and development costs from taxable income and depreciate the cost of capital equipment as do most modern tax systems. It is clear that, again on the Anglo-American model, there is a clear separation between tax accounting and accounting for financial reporting (Article 42).

It is not obvious why Kazakstan should want to use this system. The disconnection between tax and accounting in the USA and UK arose primarily because of a demand for financial information by capital markets which meant that tax-based numbers are not appropriate. The issue is whether or not in Kazakstan the main purpose of accounting is to serve the needs of capital markets or to ensure that the state captures the appropriate amount of taxation. If it is the latter then this implies, for tax audit purposes, that there is a transparency between the numbers recorded in a business's accounting plan (with an associated chart of accounts) as is used in France, Spain, Greece and now Romania) may be an appropriate way of obtaining this transparency.

What gave all changes in the fiscal policy to the national economy? By the end of 1995 income from taxes increased 6.2 per cent compared to the forecast, including such taxes as VAT, income tax from judicial bodies, income tax from physical bodies, and excises on 11.1 per cent.

But for 1996 the situation changed. The volume of budget assets was planned as 18.4 per cent of GDP, which could be explained through the cancellation of a lot of non-tax income, decreasing the tax rate on profit. But at the same time it was supposed to increase the rate for VAT, import (customs, tariffs), etc. Besides this, in 1996 the government proposed to cut the non-payment of wages, the extinction of debts of leading enterprises through the transfer rights of management under the jurisdiction of foreign companies and other measures.

The main barrier is non-collection of taxes. For example, the main types of taxes not collected in the first part of 1996 were: VAT – 33.1 per cent, income tax on profit of – juridical bodies – 52.6 per cent, excises – 63.2 per cent, etc. Of the projected income from taxes, – 78.9 per cent was not collected, and such a large scale of uncollected taxes is a consequence of serious deficiencies of the tax system, a lack of effective instruments of tax collection and/ or corruption.

The new law about tax relations is concerned with realisation of only one function of taxes, fiscal, and completely ignores the stimulative and regulative functions of taxes in the economy. The total rate of taxes, as managers of enterprises confirm, is still very high. Rates of taxes were not diversified and therefore do not reflect priorities of the economy.

Of course it is very difficult to call the taxation of investment goods of high VAT with the high import tax, which are in deficit in the Kazakstani economy, a positive feature of the Tax Code. From our point of view the calculation of VAT needs reconsideration. A rate of VAT calculated from the total amount of prices, excise and customs and collection and results in double taxation. All this stimulates the growth of prices, maintaining and perpetuating the high level of inflation.

Besides this, in the taxation of export goods VAT is using a double principle: with foreign countries using the zero rate, and CIS countries not. The last position is beneficial to countries which export more goods (for example for Russia, which has a substantial positive net export balance with Kazakstan).

The law, while based on the principle of fairness, simplicity and improving taxation, liquidated all tax exemptions in the economy. But on the other hand, taxation was not improved.

The new tax law did not stabilise the tax system of Kazakstan. In December 1995 changes were put in the Tax Code which established 10 per cent tax exemption for free economic zones. The President questioned some tax exemptions for small and medium business, foreign investors.

The Tax Law did not solve the problem of optimal taxes' distribution between central and local budgets and taxation to these budgets.

All these factors decrease the income part of the budget, that leads to increasing internal debt and non-payments of wages, making a higher budget deficit and inflation.

INTER-ENTERPRISE ARREARS

The achievement of macroeconomic stabilisation would not necessarily lead to the automatic recovery of the economy. The new challenge is to achieve economic growth without allowing a rise in, or a new wave of inflation. What makes an already extraordinarily difficult task for the Kazakstani government even more complicated is not the problem of halting inflation, but how to do so without an increase in the decline in production. This apprehension has a real presence, and will be of great importance for the next three or four years. Due to the stabilisation policy, domestic demand for goods and services, (which is a necessary condition for economic growth), has been reduced to a catastrophically low level. Artificial or compulsory limitation of population incomes is a 'double edged sword'. Of course such a policy could be effective for halting pure inflation, but on the other hand this policy strongly limits the demand for goods and services, and without such a demand supply cannot exist. This problem is not only a macroeconomic problem, but of course is connected with a lack of policy regarding income, saving and consumption, with a high level of unemployment as well as a crisis of non-payments constituting a very real tragedy for Kazakstani economy. This crisis limits the monetary income of the population, increasing overdue debts on salaries and on other social payments.

In 1994 for example, of the total Kazakstani industrial decline (28.5 per cent), only 3 per cent was connected to the narrowing sales market, and the other 25.5 per cent resulted from financial problems. According to calculations by the Centre for Euro-Asian Studies (Reading, UK), in 1994 26 per cent of the rise in Kazakstani prices was caused by inter-enterprise arrears, and for the first half of 1995, it resulted in more than 54 per cent. This provides persuasive evidence of the fact that inflation was totally dependent on inter-enterprise arrears. Artificial suppression of the inflation level of the Kazakstani economy alters the realistic vision of the situation and delays economic restructuring. Inter-enterprise arrears are largely the consequence of the way in which a serious downturn affects an unreformed financial system. If sectoral decline coincides with highly expansionary fiscal policy (resulting partly from subsidising of unprofitable firms) and/or monetary policy (either to finance fiscal deficits or to refinance commercial banks afflicted with bad loans), the result is inflation. Such a situation exists in the Kazakstani case. In this situation, if such a decline is accompanied by tight monetary and fiscal policy but not by tight budget constraints, the result is a build-up of arrears. Ickes and Ryterman (1992; 1993) discuss such explanations for the rapid build-up of arrears in the early 1990s as the malfunctioning of the rouble zone, the high real cost of credit obtained from other sources (causing disintermediation), the changing composition of aggregate (especially government) demand, the aggregate demand shock caused by the infamous 'cash shortage', and tax avoidance *vis-à-vis* the new value-added tax.

By the end of June 1996 8000 enterprises and organisations had overdue debts on salaries to the total amount of Tenge 43 billion or 39 per cent of June GDP. In June 1996 total monthly wages in Kazakstan were Tenge 26.4 billion, wages arrears were Tenge 43 billion, which means that wages were not paid for 50 days. Therefore the first prioritised problem arose immediately – recovery of the domestic demand through the increasing population income and state budget, without which the recovery of the economy would not take place. It is necessary to remark that through the export of raw materials it would be impossible to compensate for a decrease in domestic demand. Through the experience of the Eastern and Central European countries it is possible to conclude that economic recovery in the first post-stabilisation years was through the slackening of the limits to demand.

The obvious question might be how is it possible to achieve? The simple answer will be through the paying off of overdue debts on salaries, pensions, subsidies, etc. But at the same time the dangers of the new high level of inflation are evident. In addition, this question could be solved only in the event of a halt in the crisis of arrears in general, which is a specific feature of a post-socialist economy: inter-enterprise arrears, arrears between commercial banks and enterprises; arrears between enterprises and budget. From 1994 the volume of arrears grew most rapidly. In 1995 this figure was increased by 608 per cent and became 22 per cent of GDP. By the end of 1996 the total arrears were 35 per cent of GDP.

The speed of the increase in arrears was higher than the change in the increase in inflation, therefore arrears are saving the inflation potential and increasing inflation expectations. In addition, at the present time arrears have become the main factor, which has the effect of halting production growth, destabilising the budget and bank systems. Debts payable were more than 1.9 times higher than debts receivable by the end of 1996. Through this indicator it is necessary to conclude that all sectors of the

Kazakstani economy are insolvent (except communications enterprises, where debts receivable are higher than debts payable – 10.6 billion. Tenge and 4.0 billion Tenge respectively – (see Table 6.4).

Debts of Kazakstani enterprises to enterprises in other CIS countries and enterprises of non-CIS countries are more than four times higher than the respective debts of these enterprises to the Kazakstani enterprises. More than 17.9 per cent of the overdue debts payable are payments to the budget, and 4.5 per cent of these debts are payments for bank credits.

One of the larger debtors is the state itself. According to the Kazakstani Statistical Office, of the total volume of the buyers' debts receivable, the state share is 13–15 per cent, from this figure overdue arrears are more than 60 per cent. The share of overdue state – arrears was 7 per cent of GDP by the first six months of 1996.

If this problem of arrears is not satisfactorily resolved, the stagnation of the economy will inevitably take place in Kazakstan. It would be impossible to achieve recovery of the economy, even with a more or less appropriate level of inflation, because the economy and population cannot continue to exist in the future in such strained monetary conditions caused by non-payable arrears. The number of unprofitable enterprises reached more than 50 per cent of the total number of the Kazakstani enterprises in 1996 (i.e. the number increased by more than 18 per cent). In Figure 6.6 we can see the dynamic of the growth of inter-enterprise arrears in Kazakstani enterprises, such that in December 1996 the net debts were Tenge 497.7 billion, when in December 1995 the net debts were Tenge 225.7 billion.

Table 6.4   Debts payable and debts receivable (bil Tenge) on 1 December 1996 by sectors of economy

	Debts receivable	*Debts payable*	*Net debts*
Total	533.6	1 011.1	477.5
Industry	259.6	599.0	339.4
Agriculture	21.6	133.4	111.8
Transport	44.9	46.1	1.2
Communications	10.6	4.0	–6.6
Construction	55.7	59.7	4.0
Trade	12.7	26.7	14.0
Other sectors	128.5	142.2	13.7

Source: Socialno-cconomicheskoe polozhenie Respubliki Kazakhstan, 1997: 24.

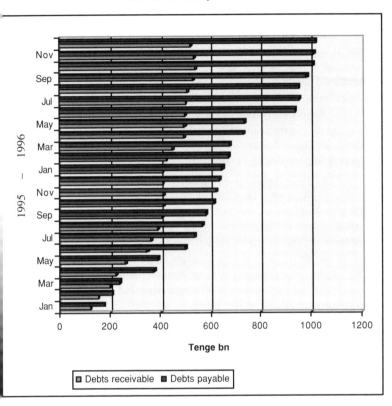

Figure 6.6   Enterprise sector arrears, 1995–96 (Tenge billion) (*Source*: Figure was created based on *Kazakstan Economic Trends*, First Quarter 1996: Table 11.1 and *Kazakstan Economic Trends*, January 1997: Table 11.1)

By the end of December 1996 wages arrears by state, private and partially state-owned firms, ranged Tenge 47.9 billion, 35.8 per cent of GDP of this month, according to *Kazakstan Economic Trends*. In many oblasts workers did not receive any wages for up to 10 months. From the total amount of wages arrears on 1 December 1996, nearly half of this amount (Tenge 24.6 billion) were enterprises with mixed forms of property without foreign participation; nearly 36 per cent (Tenge 6.4 billion) were state enterprises; 13 per cent (Tenge 6.4 billion) were private enterprises, and more than 2 per cent (Tenge 1.1 billion) were enterprises with foreign and mixed forms of property. (Socialno-Economicheskoe Polozhenie Respubliki Kazakhstan za yanvar-dekabr 1996 goda).

Some separate actions of the Kazakstani Government had the effect of slowing down the changes in the growth of arrears, but did not solve the overall problem. In the *Programme of Governments Activity in Increasing Reforms and Recovery from the Economic Crisis* (1994) the government suggested solving this problem by means of the enterprises bankruptcy law and circulation of bills. But the Kazakstani government implemented all these inadequate laws poorly. The bankruptcy law has only been app-lied in extreme circumstances (for example the Kazakstan Airlines or *Karmetkombinat* cases). But again it is necessary to remember that mass bankruptcy of enterprises will inevitably lead to mass unemployment and economic collapse. As was mentioned before, more than 50 per cent of enterprises are unprofitable, therefore socio-economic damage is very difficult to predict, and the consequences of such measures may well be tremendously negative. The *1996–98 Action Programme for the Deepening of Reforms* emphasises the need to improve the work of registration-analytical work, co-ordination by the government records of 'mutual requirements by the enterprises strictly on the voluntary base outside of the system of the direct or non-direct budget responsibilities', as well as 'the reforms of enterprises, regime of sanitation and bankruptcy, which allowed decrease debts through the sales of enterprises and their properties' (*The Programme of Activity of the Government for the Improvement of the Reforms on 1996–1998*, 1996: 22). But again all these projects remain projects. In any case these attempts would be unable to both solve this problem and allow an increase in economic growth.

It seems that the problem of inter-enterprise arrears in Kazakstan cannot be solved simply on the macroeconomic level, because on the one hand the Kazakstani government is unable to do anything to solve this problem (and are convinced that restrictive monetary policy may stop inflation and the accumulation of arrears, which are positively correlated with each other), and on the other hand the macroeconomic level cannot be allowed to explain the causes of the continuing build-up of arrears. The solution may be on the microeconomic level, when enterprises due to industrial relations make credible commitments for creditors and subsequently assume the respons-ibility to repay debts back in within a definite time period, otherwise there is provision for legislative punishment of errant enterprises. The governance of enterprises could be allowed to co-ordinate inter-enterprise relations, as well as to find new and credible industrial partners. Even, perhaps, to create a market of mutual inter-enterprise arrears. It is necessary to say that at the present time the process of liquidation of arrears is very painful for the Kazakstani economy, to solve the problem by radical measures is imposs-ible, and the solution could be a slow recovery on the micro level, with very careful participation on the part of the government.

IV

Other Sectors of the Reform Process and Socio-Economic Implications

IV

Other Sectors of the Reform
Process and Socio-Economic
Implications

7 Breaking New Ground

The transformation of the economy requires the creation of new dimensions of economic activity. New strength in the development of small businesses is an historically original concept for Kazakstan.

There is no doubt that there are some obstacles which can slow down the speed of the creation of a new economic sector, but nevertheless there is a point that small business could help with the problem of employment as well as might bring a necessary element to the reanimation of the economy. The effectiveness of an economy depends on the quality of co-ordination. It is obviously more important under conditions of transition that market aids the decentralisation of the co-ordination process.

It is time for the economy to create a comparative advantage which would allow Kazakstan to find its own place in the world market. There is a set expression 'Kazakstan – big potential – mineral resources – oil and gas'. The key point here is how far potential and reality? Would it be easier for Kazakstan to explore the possibility to become an oil and gas state? Due to geopolitical circumstances the solution might be vice versa. Clearly, the destiny depends upon the political decision (governmental policy).

The new banking system which is supposed to help the whole economy has begun to be created in Kazakstan. The adopted Anglo-American model of banking could allow a rational credit policy and clear institutional division of different types of bank activities, that of course will be allowed to have a specialisation and concentration. Nevertheless there is an inability to assess the lack of collateral on which the loans are secured and uncertainty about the legal framework; all of these are problems commercial banks confront in their lending activity.

DEVELOPMENT OF SMALL AND MEDIUM BUSINESS

The non-state sector of the Kazakstani economy is functioning less effectively than was projected, due to the realisation of the privatisation programme and development of the programme of supporting entrepreneurship. It was defined by the continuing economic crisis which is taking place in the economy of Kazakstan.

The decline in production of the non-state sector was more visible than the decline in industry as a whole. In some respects it was predictable, as

121

the majority of privatised enterprises are small and medium size enterprises, which are more sensitive to the economic changes (due to quite limited potential sources). The base of the non-state sector is small and medium enterprise, as well as the creation of entrepreneurship.

This type of business is very important, as the Kazakstani government is aiming to solve some social problems, particularly to create additional working places, as well as the targets to create the effective national economy, small and medium business.

The governmental policy regarding small and medium business was not substantial enough to support the new class of producers. The principle document issued by the government was the *State Programme of Supporting Entrepreneurship*, which was aimed at creating full state support enterprises for the small and medium businesses in: legislative, informational-analytical, foreign economic, taxation, finance and credit, and staff training. Due to the inefficient activity of the state executive organs, key points in this programme were not run as scheduled.

By 1993–94 the new programme of state support and development entrepreneurship was put into place. The new programme was different from previous programmes only in some small and inconsequential aspects. One of the disadvantages of the programme was the unrealistic estimation of the development of small and medium business. For example, the projection of the programme was to create a total of 150 000 small and medium businesses. In addition it was particularly naïve to think that small businesses would be able to produce 70 per cent of the total agricultural production, 40 per cent of the total industrial production, and 90 per cent of total services and trade as soon as 1996. These figures were not realistic, even in developed countries it would be difficult to find such proportions. Generally, the programme has a content which can be characterised as *conceptual points*, which of course should not be allowed to estimate the efficiency of the proposed activities.

In 1993 the number of co-operatives decreased by 1850 which was only 40 per cent of the 1992 total, and the number of workers decreased by 54 800 employees (56 per cent of 1992). In 1993 the number of small enterprises sharply increased by 3400 enterprises, and at the same time the number of employees decreased by 27 500.

In 1994 2049 co-operatives, 12 200 small enterprises and 18 673 private enterprises were functioning in Kazakstan, with 344 000 employees (6.1 per cent of the total labour source in Kazakstan). In 1994, according to the *Indicative List of Investment Projects* for small and medium business, the government was planning to provide US$ 250 million in guarantees. But due to the danger of increasing external debt, the Kazakstani government announced a moratorium on such support, and the current share of production of small and medium business is 1.3 per cent of the total industrial production.

During the last two years the small and medium enterprises have had to cut activity, due to a lack of investment and capital. In reality the level of production produced by the co-operatives has been decreasing, and at the same time the number of private enterprises running commercial activities has been on the increase.

Non-sufficient governmental financial support of small business led to its concentration in the industrially-developed regions of Kazakstan, whilst in the regions which are agricultural production orientated the number of small enterprises is significantly smaller.

When enterprises are registered as small enterprises, they include one dimension of activity, but in reality they are mostly engaged in commercial (trade, as opposed to production) activities. This can be explained through the interest rate on credits, which is at such a level that it is practically impossible to have effective production and only commercial activity will provide the necessary return for repayments. In 1992–95 the commercial banks provided only short-term credits directed particularly at commercial activity.

Therefore the main reasons for the low efficiency of production and the decrease in entrepreneurial activity in small and medium business are the following:

- a negative economic situation;
- an unsatisfactory criminal environment;
- a lack of necessary, and ineffective existing legislative documents, which are strongly coherent between each other;
- a taxation policy which does not assist small businesses.

According to *The 1996–98 Action Programme for the Deepening of Reforms* the main priority for 1996–98 is the microeconomic sphere. The role of small and medium business became a primary target, but of course this would depend upon the general economic climate (such as investment policy, taxation, etc.) as well as upon coherent and logical governmental support.

THE KAZAKSTANI COMPARATIVE ADVANTAGE: OIL AND GAS

After obtaining independence, Kazakstan became one of the most promising regions for world oil companies. Kazakstan possesses extensive deposits of crude oil and natural gas, with proven deposits amounting to 2 billion tonnes of oil and 1100 billion cubic metres of gas. The estimates regarding the Kazakstani reserves are 3.5 billion tonnes of oil and 2 trillion cubic metres of gas. Nevertheless Kazakstan has never been a major producer of hydrocarbons because of the legacy of the labour specialisation in the FSU. The majority of the oil producing regions in Kazakstan are in the western regions of Atyrau, Mangistau, Uralsk and Actybinsk. The most difficult problem is refineries: one of the refineries is located in Atyrau, and two others in Pavlodar (North Kazakstan) and Shimkent (Eastern Kazakstan). The latter two refineries are not connected by a pipeline to the West, and as a result receive their raw materials from western Siberia via the Omsk pipeline. There are major oil deposits in western Kazakstan bordering the Caspian Sea. In 1993 the government of Kazakstan signed an agreement with Chevron Oil Company to explore and develop the Tengiz field under the Tengischevroil joint venture (TCO). The agreement was that Chevron would make substantial investments by 1997, but the latest information demonstrates that the political debates between LUKoil, Tengizmunaigas and Chevron constitute a significant problem for the realisation of this project.

The dynamic of oil production is presented in Figure 7.1. The production of oil increased over the latter half of the 1980s, from 18.656 million tonnes in 1980 to 26.951 million tonnes in 1991. By 1994 the output of crude oil had fallen to 20.279 million tonnes, and production of natural gas had declined to 4488 million cubic meters (Figure 7.2).

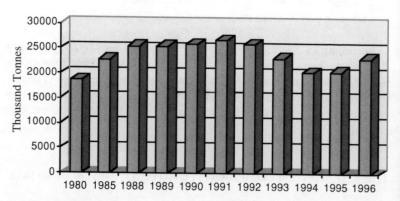

Figure 7.1 Production in the oil industry, 1980–96 (*Source*: *Statisticheskii Ezhegodnik Kazakhstana, 1991, 1995, 1996, 1997*)

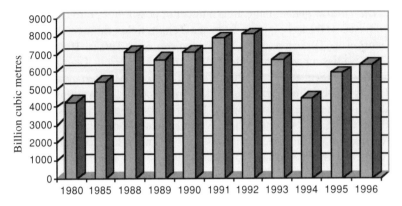

Figure 7.2 Production in the natural gas industry, 1980–96 (*Source: Statisticheskii Ezhegodnik Kazakhstana, 1991, 1995, 1996, 1997*)

The problem with oil production for Kazakstan is the difficulty with transportation to the international market, because the country has no export pipeline of its own. There are only two possible methods for Kazakstan at present: export through the Russian oil pipeline system (but in this case Russia would be a competitor with Kazakstan), or reach agreement with Iran. Like Russia, in the case of quick development of the Kazakstani oil sector, Iran would also consider Kazakstan a competitor. Therefore on the one hand it is very important for Kazakstan to have its own set of export pipelines, but on the other hand this set will increase the already high costs of the oil sector as well as complicating what is an already complex situation between all the Central Asian Republics and their neighbours. At the beginning the Kazakstani government had at least 12 possible export pipelines options, the most realistic being Russian, Turkish, Iranian and Eastern.

The Russian option: there was a suggestion that the Caspian Pipeline Consortium (CPC) (shareholders include the government of Russia, Oman and Kazakstan and the oil companies Mobil, Chevron, Oryx (USA), Agip (Italy), British Gas, LUKoil and Rosneft (Russia) should build the 750 km pipeline from Tengiz fields through Novorossysk (Black Sea coast, Russia) at a cost of US$ 1 billion. But there are some obstacles facing Kazakstan here, the first being financial difficulties for this project between Kazakstan and Russia. Russia can possibly restrict future Kazakstani oil exports through Russian territory to prevent the Kazaks from decreasing oil prices. It would be incredibly difficult for Kazakstan to curtail future exports as Kazakstan already has a significant shortage of hard currency revenue.

The Turkish option: there are a number of possibilities through the CPC proposed 1600 km pipeline from the Tengiz fields through Russia and Georgia to Turkey and the Mediterranean Sea; Tefken Holding A.S. (Turkey) has a project to build a 1900 km pipeline from Tengiz, through the Caspian Sea, across Azerbaijan and Iran, to the Mediterranean coast of Turkey via the already existing Turkey-Iran pipeline. Such options are less attractive than the Russian option because first of all it is less commercially viable, and secondly there is an element of political risk: Georgia, Azerbaijan are unstable territories, etc. (even Turkey has had constant conflicts with the Kurdish Workers' Party).

The Iranian option: this project cannot be realistic because the proposed 800 km pipeline from the Aktau fields, across the Caspian Sea via Azerbaijan and Iran is contrary to both governmental and private industrial US interests. The major obstacle here is finance, which Iran cannot provide, but the US opposes Iran receiving multilateral financing. Iran considers Kazakstan a potential competitor, and can restrict Kazakstani oil exports. Nevertheless, 'Kazakhstan [*sic*] and Azerbaijan have both signed agreements for Tehran to buy their oil and then export an equal amount of its own oil through its ports on the Persian Gulf or Indian Ocean.' (Starr, 1997: 29) By 1997 the agreement on the location swap with Iran had began. The first shipment of 15 000 tons of crude oil from Kazakstan to Iran was dispatched.

The Eastern option: there is a potential to propose pipelines through Afghanistan, Pakistan or China, but all of them are quite costly and in the near future cannot be considered realistic options.

Another crucial problem which Kazakstan has is a lack of refineries, without which the country cannot position itself as an exporter of oil, because Kazakstani crude oil contains many impurities and this could even lead to a substantial environmental hazard.

In the gas sector significant partners for Kazakstan are British Gas and Agip (both of which hold a 42.5 per cent equity) and the Russian partner state-owned gas monopoly Gasprom (15 per cent equity). At the present time Karachganak (the largest natural gas field with estimated reserves of more than 1 trillion cubic metres) depends heavily upon Gasprom and continues to have huge losses in export of raw materials. The real efficiency of Karachaganak would be dependent upon the building of its own refineries.

The question of oil and gas constituting a comparative advantage for the Kazakstani economy is a complex one. The problems and obstacles here are not only economical but also geopolitical. Participation in the Caspian question[1] is making the Kazakstan position unsustainable at present. The future development (in which respect and with whom) of the potential Kazakstani comparative advantage (at least in the foreseeable future) will continue to be primarily dependent upon the formation of political agreements.

STRATEGY OF THE BANKING SYSTEM

In banking reform Kazakstan had two main tasks. First of all to build an independent institution – the National Bank of Kazakstan – which would be able to formulate and conduct a monetary policy for Kazakstan.

A much larger and more complicated problem was the creation of commercial banks. The confusion and uncertainty following independence created an environment in which many new Kazakstani banks emerged spontaneously.

Kazakstan has had a two-tier banking system since the end of the 1980s. The two tiers consist of: the State Bank of Kazakstan (with its network of 19 regional branches and local payment settlement centres); whilst the lower level is represented by the commercial banks.

This process began when Kazakstan was a part of the USSR, when two major banks were created: *Gosbank* and *Stroybank*. Stroybank provided the foundation for the creation of three other banks in 1987: *Promstroibank* (at the present time part of the Turan Alem Bank), *Agroprombank* and *Zhilstroibank*.

The foundation in 1990 of a branch of the *Vnesheconombank* (USSR) gave Kazakstan the ability to service foreign bank operations.

The period from 1992 to 1993 was a period during which the National Bank of Kazakstan adopted some of the functions of the Central Bank, and there was much formation and development of commercial banks.

In monetary terms, independence essentially began when Kazakstan left the rouble zone, and the National Bank (previously Gosbank – the Soviet State Bank) became responsible for national currency issue, the imposition of reserve requirements, the refinancing of commercial banks, and lending to the government. By 1994 Kazakstan had 210 banks, the prevalent mood in business circles being that it was necessary to own a bank to be in business, and not only was it very easy to establish a bank, it was also very attractive in terms of raising credits. Consequently, the combination of banks with low levels of capital, and the step by step criminalisation and mismanagement of the business banking system led to the discrediting of the banking system in the public view.

Effective independence for the banking system was not realised until March 1995, when the National Bank of Kazakstan was removed from governmental and parliamentary supervision by presidential decree.

Relations between central banks and governments differ in their nature, scope and direction, with the principal influencing factors being the prevailing political conditions, the dominant politico-economic theory of the time, and the exchange-rate regimes. Whilst an exchange rate regime may be chosen to force fiscal discipline on future governments, fiscal discipline enables a greater choice of exchange rate regime. In general, the fiscal stance determines the viable choice of exchange rate regimes, which in turn determines the consistent set of monetary policies. Given this, even the most independent central bank is still constrained by the prior choices of fiscal stance and exchange rate regime.

Interest rate controls could be designed to prevent potentially harmful cut throat competition, to discourage excessive money and credit expansion, to stimulate investment in priority sectors, and to raise revenue for the government at below-market rates of interest.

The relationship between the government and the National Bank of Kazakstan was problematic, and since 1992 the National Bank has been obliged to undertake various additional actions such as:

- rescuing insolvent financial institutions;
- using selective credit policies to provide subsidised credit to agriculture;
- using selective credit policies to provide subsidised credit for developing financial institutions; and
- providing exchange rate guarantees or subsidies for essential imports and debt servicing.

The banking sector in Kazakstan is providing a reason for concern regarding the long-term stability of the system. Central to this concern is the fact that the activities of the National Bank are both very large, and to a large extent impenetrable to outside analysis. Difficulties arise with issues such as measurement of contingent liabilities, the accounting conventions used, valuation calculations (particularly of foreign policy-denominated claims), and most crucial and fundamental of all, the demarcation between fiscal and monetary activities.

This relationship is central to economic policy. In order to determine the degree of independence of the Central Bank, a number of determinants are generally accepted, but it is very difficult to reduce these to a single denominator, and in the case of the National Bank of Kazakstan, particularly difficult to apply. For example, the ownership, and thus the right to enjoy profits, is clouded, as is the relationship in terms of key appointments. A brief list of the appointment and ownership structure as advised by the National Bank is as follows:

	Before 1995	*After 1995*
Central Bank ownership	State	State
Distribution of Central Bank profits	Parliament	President
Governor appointed by	Parliament	President
Governor appointed on proposal of …	President	President
Deputy Governors appointed by …	Parliament	President
Tenure of Central Bank officers, Governor (and Deputy Governors)	Six years	Six years

The presidential decree of 31 August 1995, *About Banks and Banking Activity in the Republic of Kazakstan*, was aimed at reducing the ease at which banks had been set up previously. The amount necessary to establish a new bank was set as the equivalent of US$ 500 000, in addition to other measures aimed at reducing the increase in banks with a limited future, such as publication of annual reports including a balance sheet and profits and losses in a form established by the Central Bank. Each bank's accounting director had to be approved by the National Bank. Banks of the second tier were divided into two categories: (a) deposit banks and (b) investment banks.

By 1995 the banking system in Kazakstan consisted of 130 commercial banks, including six large groups of banks: state, inter-states, joint stock banks with governmental participation, private, foreign and joint banks.

On 1 January 1997 there were 101 banks of the second level, including one interstate bank, five state banks and eight banks with foreign participants. In addition ten foreign banks had established offices in Kazakstan. At the present time the consolidation of banks is very important for Kazakstan.

The annual rate of inflation reached 1000 per cent throughout 1992 to 1994, peaking at close to 2000 per cent in the middle of 1994. From 1995 the monetary policy of the National Bank of Kazakstan was tightly restricted, and the annual inflation began a steady fall in June 1996. The annual rate of inflation in January 1996 was 53.3 per cent whilst the same figure from January 1997 is 26.2 per cent. The fall in inflation does not necessarily indicate a fundamental improvement in the economic conditions. The pessimistic view would be based on the situation with inter-enterprise arrears as well as the uncertainty in the solution for this problem on the macro level. Will the National Bank increase money supply or will the policy remain strict?

It is the responsibility of the National Bank of Kazakstan (NBK) to supervise the banking system. The banking supervision department of the NBK was created in late 1993 and it was some time before proper prudential regulations was established, for example, in 1993 only 10 per cent of the commercial banks had satisfied the prudential requirements.

In 1995 the environment for banks changed with the introduction of regulations regarding the central bank and banking activity[2] as well as the NBK tightening the regulations regarding commercial banks:

- Introduction of new loan classification schemes, so as to reduce the level of concealment of non-performing loans;
- Internal provision for non-performing loans was made mandatory;
- Accounting standards were introduced that were based upon international accounting rules;
- Capital standards were introduced and domestic bank supervisors issued weighting of assets and the calculation of capital guidelines; and
- The increased minimum capital requirements for new banks reduced the number of new banks.

Despite these regulatory changes, and an evident new atmosphere within Kazakstani banking circles, the fundamental problem of the credibility of banking supervision remains. The supervisors appointed do not have risk management experience, which is necessary for the level of inspection required, and the information systems put in place are ill-equipped to provide off-site surveillance. In addition, it is evident that the focus of banks is upon liquidity and other immediate issues, and long-term issues are not seen as of such importance. The lack of a sufficient legal infrastructure such as property rights, bankruptcy laws, and out-of-court settlement experience causes difficulties for consistent loan recovery.

It is essential to the entire economy, and in particular to the efficient operation of the banking sector, that a modern payment system be established in Kazakstan. It is necessary for banks to be able to pay settlements between payer and payee as quickly as possible after the payment instruction has been made. For example, during the later years of the USSR the structure was such that the cycle of clearing and settlement often took several weeks. It is also necessary that use of credit transfers (long the payment method in planned economies) be supplemented by different payment options such as cheques, payment cards etc.

Other important factors necessitating the reform of the payment system are the need to reduce the association of risk with payment, and the need to increase the efficiency of central bank monetary policy.

The reform process announced by the NBK to be in place by 1998 is based upon a two tiered payment system: an interim payment system, which would essentially rely upon central bank money for settlement, whilst utilising a large-volume transfer system over a real time computer system; and a long-term payment system which would provide the infrastructure necessary for same day settlement.

One of the suggested methods of providing banking system stability and depositor (especially small depositor) protection is to introduce deposit insurance. This reduces the chances of a run on the banks, particularly when the failure of one bank could start a chain reaction which would encompass the whole banking system. Whilst there is not a system of deposit insurance in place at the present time in Kazakstan, it is important that this be rectified. The result would be more trust in the banking system, a rise in the amount of long-term deposits (which in turn would provide stability for long-term loans to provide increased macroeconomic stability). Table 7.1 demonstrates the structure of deposits in Kazakstan.

In order for a deposit insurance scheme to be successfully put into place in Kazakstan, the following preconditions should be met:

- participation of both the government and the NBK;
- mandatory participation by all banks and other related financial institutions;
- the insurance cover need not necessarily be for the full volume of deposits; and
- the management of the insurance scheme should have adequate state funding in the initial phase, and subsequently be able to borrow for the NBK or government in the event of a crisis developing.

Table 7.1   Structure of money in Kazakstan (end of period)

	1990[a]	1991	1992	1994[b]	1995
Currency in circulation	6 580	13 959	154 271	20 255	47 998
Deposits[c]	21 234	69 875	533 185	33 673	68 601
Money (M2)	27 814	83 334	687 456	53 928	116 599
Deposits to Money (M2) (%)	76.3	83.8	77.6	62.3	58.8

[a] Rb million in 1990–92.
[b] Tenge million in 1994–95.
[c] Demand and time deposits.

Source: The Economist Intelligence Unit Country Profile, Kazakstan, various tables, 1995–96 and *Statistical Bulletin* of the National Bank of Kazakstan, 1995, No. 1; 1996, No. 5.

The debt problem in Kazakstan involves different sectors of the economy, such as the banking sector and the industrial sector. By the end of 1993 the problem of bad debts had increased by the substantial growth in competition between commercial banks which resulted in lending increasing in risk. According to statistics from the NBK, 11.3 per cent of commercial banks short-term loans in 1994 were non-performing (National Bank of Kazakstan *Statistical Bulletin*, 1995 No. 1: 20). By the beginning of 1996, non-performing loans were approximately 39.3 per cent of the total short-term loans (National Bank of Kazakstan *Statistical Bulletin*, 1996 No. 5: 20).

The weaknesses in accounting and banking laws described earlier make it difficult to estimate the true size of the bad debt problem. There is a suggestion, however, that the problem may be diminishing, and of little long-term or structural danger.

Part of the bad debt problem stems from the fact that the major bank creditors remain state-owned enterprises. The privatisation of the state sector has been one of asset privatisation, not of organised state-owned businesses, and bank credit has played a very small role in this process. The change in the structure of bank credits since 1993 indicates that the importance of state-owned enterprises will decrease in the long term, which should in turn reduce the problem of bad debts. Long-term credits of commercial banks in the economy of Kazakstan increased from 5 per cent in 1993 to 27.5 per cent of total credits at the end 1995. More than 90 per cent of long-term credits were foreign currency credits, whilst domestic currency credits were given as short-term loans (for self-liquidating working capital).

Observations of the banking system of Kazakstan are that Kazakstan has adopted the Anglo-American model of banking system, where finance is equity-financing. From our perspective such a model is problematic for a transitional period, especially given the main disadvantage of the non-ability of banks to exert influence upon non-performing loans. The main result of the adoption of such a model in Kazakstan is the separation of deposit banks from investment banks and the impossibility for deposit bank input as resources for the enterprise shares. These weaknesses lend weight to the opinion that Kazakstan might be better suited to the European model as opposed to the Anglo-American model. Nevertheless, besides the disadvantages, Kazakstan has developed an institutional base and organisational structures, human capital and some financial resources. The overall picture is that of the innate ability to develop a banking system which will lend stability and an infrastructure for economy-wide growth.

EXTERNAL DEBT

According to NBK estimates, Kazakstan's total external debt rose from US$ 1973.8 million in 1993 to US$ 4081.4 million by the first quarter of 1997 (Table 7.2). The share of external debt guaranteed by the government of the Republic of Kazakstan within the total external debt is more than 70 per cent. More than 56 per cent of this amount are loans received from official creditors, more than 35 per cent is trade credits and 9 per cent are state securities, including Eurobonds, which were issued at the end of 1996. The Kazakstani national share of the USSR's debt (3.89 per cent) was assumed by Russia in return for Kazakstan relinquishing any present or future claim(s) to the central assets of the USSR.

External debt by creditors continues to rise. The IMF and the World Bank continue to support Kazakstan, and obviously the share of debt to international organisations is still growing. The government provides debt servicing to the medium and long term debt. The spread of repayments of both existing and anticipated debt is reasonable, despite a certain level of 'bunching' in 1998 and particularly in 1999 as grace periods expire. Servicing this debt is not a particularly difficult burden, as the levels are reasonably low.

Table 7.2 Gross external debt (US$ millions, end of period)

	Total			of which			
		Direct government and guaranteed	Share %	Non-guaranteed	Share %	Inter-enterprise arrears*	Share %
1993	1 973.8	1 765.6	89.5	0.0	0.0	208.2	10.5
1994	3 258.4	2 715.8	83.3	0.0	0.0	542.6	16.7
1995	3 167.0	2 050.5	64.7	145.4	4.6	971.1	30.7
1996	3 741.0	2 621.5	70.1	217.2	5.8	902.3	24.1
1997							
I	4 081.4	2 637.5	64.6	267.9	6.6	1 176.0	28.8

* December 1993 – National Bank of Kazakstan: from December 1994 – National Statistical Agency

Source: National Bank of Kazakstan estimates, Quarterly publication.

Debt management and uncertainty as to the true intentions of the authorities are the major debt problems for Kazakstan. The problem with arrears is wider than simply the lack of record keeping, control or monitoring. This problem mainly concerns the behaviour of the government, which tried to refuse obligations undertaken in its name by ministries and other official bodies. The record of the last years has been discouraging. Mismanagement and miscommunication between official borrowers has led to further arrears.

8 Sectors in Transition

Clearly transformation is the process of liberalisation of economic activity, in particular a programme of privatisation leading to changes in all sectors of the economy. The experiences of the CIS have shown that it is difficult to describe the process of transition and subsequent development with reference to a single model. The main problem of the failure of some *transitional models* is mostly political rather than social or even economic.

The profile of the agrarian sector was completely changed after the process of privatisation. The decrease in agricultural production during the last two years is very disturbing, especially in livestock.

Foreign economic activity, which is another sector of the Kazakstani economy, is developing in a different manner at the present time, covering not only the CIS countries but also trying to find a place for Kazakstan in world trade. The difficulties of estimation of the real figures of export and import are connected with the non-estimated suitcase trade which is very popular in Kazakstan.

All aspects of transition could not have a full description without a precise picture in the social sphere. How the population views the course of governmental reforms is an important issue. This is the outcome and evaluation, the real measure of the success of transition. The decreasing of the belief of ordinary people that at the end the standard of living would be better makes the task for the Kazakstani government much more complicated.

THE AGRICULTURAL SECTOR OF THE NEWLY PRIVATISED ECONOMY

Kazakstan had a strong agricultural base in the period before transition. All the changes which took place in the last five years have dramatically affected the situation in the Kazakstani agrarian sector. Agricultural output in 1995 was only 53 per cent of that of 1990. In the structure of agricultural production, plant-growing was 66 per cent, livestock 34 per cent, and relatively in 1990 the same indicators were 39 per cent and 61 per cent respectively (Figure 8.1). The decline in agricultural output and disposable income has reduced overall consumption levels. In particular, the focus of consumption has shifted from livestock products towards cereals, potatoes and other vegetables. But traditionally the consumption of livestock products was 1.5 times higher than all other foodstuffs.

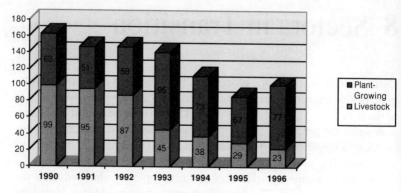

Figure 8.1 Agricultural output (in Tenge) (*Source: Selskoe khozya'istvo Respubliki Kazakhstana, 1996*: 3; *Social'no-ekonomicheskoe polozhenie respubliki Kazakhstan, 1997*: 15)

The governmental privatisation policy formulated in March 1993 ensured that every agricultural worker would receive a plot of land with a long-term hereditary rental agreement (for 99 years). This was viewed askance by the Western world, as it appeared to outsiders that Kazakstan remained ambiguous regarding their attitude towards land ownership. The legislation had, rather than deliver a concept of land ownership, established categories:

1. Permanent ownership (restricted to state enterprises);
2. Life inheritable tenure (peasant farms, household plots, gardens and dachas);
3. Permanent use;
4. Temporary use (either short term [less than 3 years], or long term [up to 99 years]); and
5. Leasing.

By April 1994, the law was extended so that land under life inheritable tenure could be transferred to non-family members, which was of course a step towards the development of a land market in Kazakstan.

By 1994, 1490 state agricultural enterprises had been privatised, which constituted two thirds of the total due to be privatised. The main aim of farm privatisation and restructuring to date has been to transform *sovkhozes* (state farms) and *kolkhozes* (collective farms), but unfortunately the legislative base for this was very weak, and there was no overall strategy or procedures in place when the privatisation began. Consequently, the process of privatisation was extremely subjective, as opposed to an economy-wide process. Prior to independence, the legislature had introduced the 1990 Law on Peasant Farms, which, although aimed at creating family farms for those wanting to become individual farmers, favoured the established hierarchy strongly.

In 1992, legislative measures were introduced in order to make the farm privatisation process more equitable. Asset shares in state farms (expressed in monetary terms) were issued, allocated on the basis of salary, years of service and professional skills. In theory, the ownership of these asset shares would allow the formation of individual (family) farms, personal contributions to stock in joint stock companies and co-operative and collective enterprises, and the ability to sell or exchange the asset shares with other shareholders. However, in real terms the effect was cosmetic. Many *sovkhozes* simply changed names, with the established hierarchy in place. Viable individual (family) farms failed to develop, as the process was particularly politicised. Whilst it is fair to say that many individual farms would not be viable due to the specialisation inherent from pre-independence, it should also be noted that the opportunity to do this was rarely presented.

The politicisation of this process was exacerbated by the Resolution of the Government no. 216 of February 1994, which allowed selected agricultural enterprises to be sold by means of closed tender. The development of the legislative base for agriculture took place in the Civil Code (March 1995), in which the basic freedom for entrepreneurship including partnership, joint stock companies and limited companies, was given to agricultural enterprises.

Prior to transition, Kazakstan had approximately 2500 large agricultural enterprises and 400 *kolkhozes*. At the present time the structure of the agricultural sector has changed towards private enterprises and non-state enterprises.

Of course it is difficult to estimate all the consequences of agrarian privatisation, but an interesting factor to emerge is the correlation between the rise in the number of non-state enterprises, and the decrease in livestock numbers (Figure 8.2). The increase in non-state enterprises was inversely proportional to the decrease in livestock. Livestock production is the single most important area in Kazakstani agriculture, as historically nomadic Kazakstani agriculture was presented in livestock terms. The use of this livestock as food in the period since independence has left low levels of stock, and Kazakstan faces a rebuilding process of not less than 15 years to restore workable levels. The supply of fodder for livestock is in decline, which is also reflected in the falling numbers (see Figure 8.3). Another problem is that livestock became a measure of payments: livestock is used to pay salaries and repay debts. According to Minister of Agriculture Serik Akhumbekov (*Kazakstanskaya pravda*, 1997, 1 March: 3) 80 per cent of the proceeds of the sale of sheep meat is barter and other payments (such as salary payment). At the same time, the situation with agricultural workers

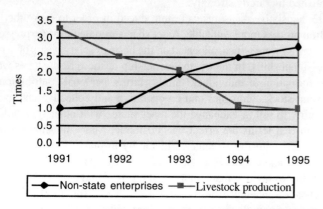

Figure 8.2 The correlation between changes in number of non-state enterprises and the decrease in animal production (*Source*: *Selskoe khozya'istvo Respubliki Kazakhstana, 1996*: 3)

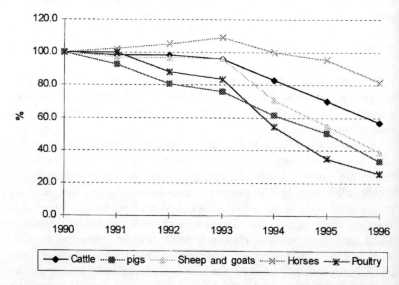

Figure 8.3 Livestock (percentage change in output) (*Source*: *Selskoe khozya'istvo Respubliki Kazakhstana, 1996*: 3. *Social'no-yekonomicheskoe polozhenie respubliki Kazakhstan, 1997*: 17)

working with this livestock has become worse since independence, as poverty levels increased. The lack of cash and care from government due to privatisation has exaggerated this situation.

The finances of the agricultural sector are in a prolonged state of deterioration. According to the state statistical office, in 1995 the number of unprofitable agricultural enterprises were 1296 units, by April 1997 this number increased up to 2593 units. The share of industrial production increased very rapidly, at the same time prices of agricultural commodities increased at a slower rate.

The delay in payments for procurement of agricultural goods as well as high inflation deprived producers of working capital. Due to the high bank interest rates, credit was difficult to obtain. The average refinancing rates of the National Bank were: 1992–65 per cent; September 1993–170 per cent; March 1994–300 per cent; and November 1995–52 per cent. The picture was not all bleak for all agricultural producers however, as the government up to 1995 allocated large amounts (30 billion Tenge in 1994) for agricultural enterprises at low interest rates. This allocation was sharply reduced in 1995 (down to 11 billion Tenge, of which 4.1 billion Tenge was for state grain purchases).

Of course the government reacted to the situation and tried to create some financial institutions such as the Agriculture Support Fund (ASF) (Resolution 1447, December 1994). The aim was for agricultural debts to be transferred to this fund. The agricultural debts amount to more than 1.1 billion Tenge (3 per cent of the total), and in 1997 the ASF is expecting to cover the last amount of the debt, some 8.7 billion Tenge. The ASF provides direct subsidies for the support of some target activities, most significantly to sheep farming and also to the livestock programme, and the promotion of the usage of elite seed. As much as 3.58 billion Tenge was allocated from the state budget to agriculture in 1996, and the Minister of Agriculture tried to determine the purposes for the use of this money.

There have been governmental efforts to provide relief for the beleaguered agricultural sector, particularly cereals. In March 1995 a promissory note issue aimed at financing purchase of 900 000 tonnes of cereals for state reserves was approved by a resolution of the Cabinet of Ministers.

Financial constraints have led to difficulties in upgrading agricultural machinery, and maintaining existing structures. This is a dynamic regardless of whether the relevant farms have undergone restructuring or not. As well as experiencing difficulties in obtaining finance to upgrade, farms also experience difficulties in obtaining the necessary equipment/buildings etc. For example, the Pavlodar Tractor Plant collapsed, and there is a particular difficulty in obtaining this type of machinery throughout Kazakstan.

Fertilisers are also a case in point. The sharp contraction in the fertiliser industry since 1991 will have a long-term effect upon future production. Whilst a short-term saving, cutting of fertiliser to the level expressed in Kazakstan (in 1995 it was estimated that less than 40 000 tonnes of non-organic fertilisers were used on an are of less than 0.3 million hectares, in comparison to the pre-reform level of about 665 000 tonnes over 9.2 million hectares) necessarily affects future production from the land. If on average from 1986–90 1 hectare of land received 26 kilos of mineral fertiliser, in the last years this volume has decreased tenfold, with a correlating drop in productivity over time (Figure 8.4).

The situation in agriculture remains in crisis. The government still needs to put a lot of effort and pressure towards the restructuring of the agricultural sector. Dynamics such as the rapid decrease in livestock numbers and the disuse of fertiliser lead us to the conclusion that the agricultural sector of Kazakstan is beset with specific long-term problems, and necessarily, long-term problems require long-term answers rather than short-term credit supplements.

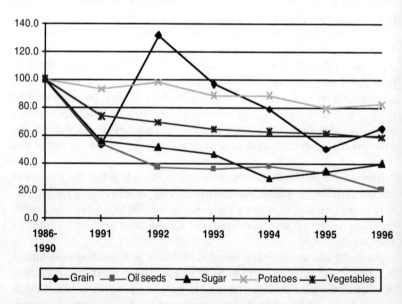

Figure 8.4 Productivity of crops, tonne/hectare (percentage change; average per year 1986–90 = 100%) (*Source: Selskoe khozya'istvo Respubliki Kazakhstana, 1996*: 3. *Social'no-ekonomicheskoe polozhenie respubliki Kazakhstan, 1997*: 16)

FOREIGN ECONOMIC ACTIVITY

The Kazak foreign trade system underwent a period of significant loosening in 1994–95. Significant areas were:

- the abolishing of the monopolies of certain state-owned foreign trade organisations;
- reduction of the list of goods subject to quotas and licensing;
- decrease in the rate of import and export tax.

However, governmental influence upon the foreign trade system remains strong (the Ministry of the Economy and Trade, the Kazak Eximbank). Kazakstan remains a long way from dynamic export-led growth, the trade balance and current account having been negative for the last five years. There is, however, a tendency towards lowering this deficit. For example, the current account deficit in 1994 was US$ 877.3 million, but had decreased to US$ 518.4 million in 1995, which is also reflected in the trade balance figures, being US$ 922.9 million and US$ 222.5 million respectively.[1]

The 1996 accounts remain in deficit – for the first three quarters of 1996 the figure are 4.6 per cent of GDP (3.1 per cent in 1995). Thus, the current account deficit is growing, and given that the economy itself is barely growing, this negative growth will become more marked if and when strong growth returns.

The commodity composition of trade is that Kazakstan is an exporter of oil and oil products. The ten most important groups of exports constitute over 80 per cent of the total exports.

This means that Kazakstan's exports are not very diversified and thus very vulnerable to price changes of these main commodities. In 1995 the overall price effect was positive, but in the case of a sudden drop, an expansion of volumes may not be sufficient to offset the price effects. The high concentration of Kazakstan's exports on a very limited number of commodities alone is already problematic. (*Kazakstan Economic Trends*, 1996: 18).

Recorded imports are still dominated by energy, machinery, food and vehicles. There are significant difficulties with calculating import data. The two problems are:

1. Data regarding food and other consumer goods. The National Bank of Kazakstan includes in the balance of payments figures unrecorded 'suitcase trade'. Due to low salaries and wage arrears, the ordinary

population, in the search for family income, travel to neighbouring countries such as Turkey, China and the United Arab Emirates to purchase consumer goods (clothes, food, shoes, etc.) and return to Kazakstan with these goods which they subsequently sell in open markets. Whilst this trade is of fiscal disadvantage to the government, it is recognised that it is an important source of income, and consequently restrictions upon cross-border traders have been significantly reduced (in January 1997 goods weighing between 70 and 270 kg had duty on them halved).

2. Data problems with recording the significant volume of barter deals which are not recorded by managers of enterprises.

Whilst the government accepts the existence of this trade upon a microeconomic level[2] it also has macroeconomics implications. This is a stable import of consumer goods which demonstrates the low competitiveness of domestic products, and in many cases the complete absence of domestic production of such goods. In addition, the lack of domestic investment is reflected in the fact that excess money is being used during the process of this trade as opposed to being invested in the Kazakstani infrastructure. It has been estimated that the *real* level of imports in 1995 (for example) could be as much as 47 per cent higher than that officially recorded. If this is applied to current figures, the trade deficit would be significantly reduced.

The former Soviet Republics continue to be Kazakstan's largest trading partners, particularly Russia (Table 8.1). Russia has a predominance in both export and import accounts, accounting for 69.7 per cent and 70.9 per cent of inter-Republican trade in 1993. Russia accounted for 58 per cent of Kazakstan's imports in 1996, and this Russian dominance appears to be increasing, particularly in the light of the treaties of integration which have been signed.

In Kazakstan's 1996 total volume of goods turnover, 62 per cent is with CIS countries (59 per cent in 1995). According to the Kazakstan National Statistical Office the main trading partners are:

	1996 (%)	1995 (%)
Russia	49	45
Uzbekistan	3	5
Ukraine	3	2
Turkmenistan	2	3
Kyrgyzstan	2	1
Belarus	2	2

Table 8.1 Balance of trade in Kazakstan, 1993–1996 (US$'000)

Country	1993		1994		1995		1996	
	Exports	Imports	Exports	Imports	Exports	Imports	Exports	Imports
Total	3 314.2	2 661.7	3 231.3	3 560.2	4 954.3	3 781.0	5 822.7	3 912.9
CIS countries								
Total	1 815.2	2 130.3	1 874.4	2 176.1	2 631.4	2 608.7	3 268.3	2 775.1
Belarus	90.9	58.2	43.9	64.1	57.4	79.8	42.4	112.9
Kyrgyzstan	41.7	56.2	59.8	104.0	73.3	30.8	101.6	84.4
Russia	1 273.8	1 416.9	1 438.9	1 292.1	2 102.6	1 854.4	2 627.0	2 187.5
Turkmenistan	38.8	188.2	25.3	277.6	51.1	241.3	29.2	169.9
Uzbekistan	126.9	218.0	117.2	276.6	159.5	268.2	190.6	82.3
Ukraine	148.2	144.4	128.0	119.8	121.4	86.7	202.6	87.8
Non-CIS countries								
Total	1 499	531.4	1 356.9	1 384.1	2 322.9	1 172.3	2 554.5	1 137.8
China	172.2	80.1	148.9	68.8	294.2	34.2	427.3	33.1
Finland	9.3	4.7	16.6	15.9	50.5	31.3	99.9	52.0
Germany	131.0	76.3	73.2	293.6	170.4	201.5	169.9	175.3
Italy	83.8	20.7	42.3	60.7	142.6	30.1	178.0	38.9
Lithuania	9.7	34.4	13.4	16.5	120.8	18.0	165.8	25.1
Netherlands	49.1	1.2	247.8	31.1	492.8	30.9	316.6	42.7
Switzerland	174.7	17.8	130.0	65.3	186.7	57.3	193.1	42.2
South Korea	45.5	8.5	60.1	67.0	91.6	43.2	177.8	74.8
Turkey	55.9	15.1	49.1	87.2	70.8	123.9	46.5	129.9
UK	96.9	18.9	64.9	66.4	111.7	82.8	223.2	69.8
USA	156.4	60.0	91.8	143.2	109.7	118.6	46.7	55.0

Source: Statisticheskii ezhegodnik Kazakhstana 1992–95; Socialno-economich-eskoe polozhenie Respubliki Kazakhstan za yanvar – dekabr 1996 goda.

In January 1996, Kazakstan and Uzbekistan suggested the formation of an Economic area, later joined by Kyrgyzstan. In particular, this agreement referred to sharing of mutual resources, but to date the restrictions of the Uzbek regime have proven barriers to implementation.

A significant share – 23 per cent (26 per cent in 1995) – of Kazakstan's 1996 foreign trade – was with Europe, particularly:

	1996	1995
	(%)	(%)
The Netherlands	4	6
Germany	3.5	4
United Kingdom	3	2
Italy	2	2
Switzerland	2	3

In January 1995 Kazakstan and the European Union signed a Partnership and Co-operation Agreement, aimed at providing a framework for co-operation across a wide spectrum of areas, and setting up a legal framework for the development of trade and investment links.

Among the countries of the Asian region (for purposes of immediate clarity I will include Turkey in this list), the share of 1996 goods turnover constituted 13 per cent (12 per cent in 1995), the most important being:

	1996	1995
	(%)	(%)
China	5	4
South Korea	3	1.5
Turkey	2	2

Trade regulations are mainly concerned with export quotas, licence import tariffs, and lists of authorised exports (which still exist in Kazakstan). Tariffs are now the major constraint, licences and quotas playing a subordinate role in cases where health and national security are directly involved. Since January 1995, the average tariff has been around 15 per cent with duties ranging from 5 to 15 per cent.

Imports have been liberalised over the last two years. Some export quotas and licence requirements have been abolished with the exception of those on drugs, weapons, explosives and pesticides. VAT on imports from CIS countries is 20 per cent, and a variety of excise taxes are payable at the border. Because VAT and excise duties are payable in the country of origin, the customs union suffers difficulties in establishing free trade upon equal terms. The volatile nature of import tariffs is problematic, combined with the quality control tests which the government requires, and which are conducted by SGS, a Swiss inspection agency.[3]

On the other side of the coin, export regulations are also going through a period of change. Recently exports have been a loss-maker as opposed to a source of income, therefore, export quotas have been done away with to a large extent. Some export regulations still exist, however, licence requirements exist for a number of commodities (as for imports).

As Kazak export prices gradually approached market prices minimum price requirements for fertilisers and metals were abolished in March 1996, those for oil products in July. Export prices for agricultural products remain regulated for the time being. Although this may be a restriction to export volumes, it still has a positive effect on export values in US dollar terms as the example of grain exports illustrates very well. (*Kazakstan Economic Trends*, Second Quarter 1996: 27).

GROSS DOMESTIC PRODUCT AND THE SOCIO-ECONOMIC IMPLICATIONS OF TRANSITION

The Kazakstani economy continues to make its slow crawl out of recession. Over the last six years Kazakstan has experienced a steep fall in output at a time when the decline in other (Eastern Europe) transitional countries' output began to diminish.

It is particularly difficult to track exact changes in the structure of the Kazakstani economy due to the statistical information available. In my analysis I used official statistics issued by the Kazak statistical agency, Goskomstat, Table 8.2 gives Goskomstat indicators of sectoral output for the period 1994–96. The most important changes are the drop in the agricultural sector, industry, construction and the rise in that of trade. The

Table 8.2   The structure of GDP (%to total),1994–96

	1994	1995	1996
GDP total	100	100	100
Industry	29.1	23.4	21.3
Construction	9.6	6.1	3.4
Agriculture	15.0	12.3	12.0
Transport and communication	11.1	10.6	9.4
Trade	12.1	17.1	18.2
Social sphere*	16.6	17.6	24.2
Banks	2.0	1.5	0.5
Taxes	3.3	4.9	5.2
Other	1.2	6.5	5.8

* Social sphere includes: health, education, culture and art, science, management, utilities.
Source: *Kratkii Statesticheskii Ezhegodnik Kazakstana, 1996, 1997*: 11.

decline in agriculture is due to privatisation and structural reasons, as well as that in 1993 and 1994 Kazakstan experienced poor weather conditions, resulting in a lower than usual grain harvest.

The dynamics of the GDP per capita in Kazakstan from 1991 demonstrate constant decline, which is connected with the decline of industrial production as well as with decreasing in the income of the population (Table 8.3, Figure 8.5).

In 1991 GDP per capita was US$ 4081, and by 1996 this indicator was only 56.3 per cent of the 1991 level. As a result Kazakstan has moved 76 places down the 1992 global human development index[4] (HDI) scale, from 53rd to 129th place. This level is seven times lower than the average world level. Such decline in real GDP per capita demonstrates the decrease in the standard of living, and of course leads to the decline of the HDI in Kazakstan in this period. The decreasing of the main components of HDI leads one to draw conclusions about the general tendency to cut the opportunities of people to live in normal conditions.

The criteria of efficiency of the social sphere are the result of improving the demographic situation (increasing life expectancy, decreasing infant mortality), and improving the standard of living. This is a partial system of

Table 8.3 GDP per capita in US$ by purchasing power parity, 1991–96

1991	1992	1993	1994	1995	1996*	1996 in % to 1991
4 081	3 612	3 214	2 442	2 271	2 296	56.3

* 1996 was calculated on the base of the *Statesticheskii Ezhegodnik Kazakstana, 1996, 1997*
Source: Kazakstan, Country Report, The Economist Intelligence Unit, 4th quarter 1996.

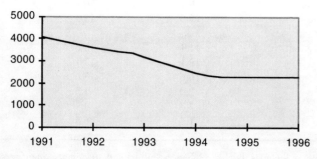

Figure 8.5 GDP per capita, 1991–96 (*Source*: Table 8.3)

indicators which would allow evaluation of one or another dimensions of the social sphere.

The standard of living is defined in comparison with the standard budget of the family, which could be minimal or optimal (rational), and is characterised by the real wage. The system of indicators which I would use for evaluating the social sphere in Kazakstan is:

- demography (number and structure of population movement);
- monetary income (such as wages, other income, entrepreneurial income, and income from rents, dividends, interest), structure of diversification and method of application;
- consumption of material goods and services;
- housing provision;
- the level of education, and the material base for science and education;
- health and the material and technological base of the health service; and
- development of culture.

At the present time all social services remain in a strong decline, due to the programme of privatisation. The main dimension of social policy in transition is the orientation of the population towards self-sufficiency and the reduction of state support to the minimum beginning with employment without housing subsidies and gradual transformation to 'user pays' services in health and education.

The dynamic of development of main indicators of the health service is characterised by a decrease in the number of doctors by 10.1 per cent (1996). The number of nurses and middle-health professionals has decreased by 25 per cent. The level of general population health is in decline, with diseases such as syphilis and tuberculosis on the increase. An economic split is beginning to appear, as private health services are available to those with the necessary means.

At the same time, the programme of the macroeconomic and financial stabilisation of the Kazakstani economy requires freezing of monetary income and wages, and a reduction in demand on the part of most of the population. In this situation income policy over the five years of reform remains a deterrent.

The Kazakstani demographic situation is a consequence of a combination of economic problems, crises in standard of living and economy, and changes in socio-political orientation. For example, the decrease in the key birth-rate indicators is a consequence of the decrease in the standard of living.

The legislative establishment of pensions presents a paradox, as life expectancy averages 61 years, and the pension scheme becomes payable on the 63rd birthday. The death rate increased between 1990 and 1995 (from 7.7 to 10.2 per thousand population), in parallel with the decrease in birth-rate. The demographic situation in Kazakstan is not defined by any one particular official government document. It is potentially hazardous not having any particular strategy for stability of the population and the labour force, and whilst there have been some official attempts to stop the decrease in population (such as monetary subsidies for families with many children, and incentives for immigration of Kazaks from nearby countries), such policies are neither stable nor efficient, and of course depend to a great deal upon economic conditions and clear governmental strategies.

The monetary income and salaries of most of the population have not kept pace with prices of consumer goods (1.3 times slower in 1991, 1.24 in 1992, 3.1 in 1993, and 1.6 in 1994). The differentiation in income and adoption of 'user pays' social services leads to a decrease in the standard of living and rudimental consumption. This process was not shared equally across the differing social and economic groups and geographical regions of Kazakstan.

The main problem of wage organisation before the period of reform was a lack of mechanism of motivation of high productivity labour. In the transitional period the situation was not changed, and in addition to the previous condition, labour became much cheaper (the share of wages in GDP decreased from 47.1 per cent in 1990 to 35.8 per cent in 1996). There are still strict labour payment regulations. The main motivation of labour became fear of losing employment, and becoming a part of mass unemployment. The average real wage is in a constant decline according to figures calculated by the Centre for Euro-Asian Studies, totalling a decrease by a factor of 4 during the period 1990–96.

Inter-sectorial and regional labour payments disproportions were created, which led to the concentration of income within the stronger groups of the population. The mass poverty of the working population began to take place and the traditionally prestigious sectors of science, the health service and education suffered (with payments 1.4–1.8 times lower than average republican payments), and the loss of this prestige is reflected in less demand for such positions. In material production the average wage is one third higher than in the non-production area, and 8 per cent higher than the average across the whole economy. The raw material sector of the Kazakstani economy has the priority in payments, whilst the best paid workers are in banks, insurance companies and credit companies. Increasingly there is also evidence of a geographical split in payment trends, with the southern oblasts (such as Zhambylsk, Taldygurgan, South Kazakstani region, and Almaty) being the worst off. Another difficulty for labour payments is wage arrears. 'On 1 February 1996 the minimum wage, under the new name of "computation index" totalled T640 ($10)' (Kazakstan Human Development Report, 1996: 51).

In the structure of monetary income, wages are the single largest determinant (more than 70 per cent). The low level of wages which define the low standard of living and low demand are connected with a lack of legislative approved minimal wages in Kazakstan, which is based upon the real cost of living, as well as a consequence of production collapse, particularly in the consumer complex. A lack of stimulus and opportunities to develop entrepreneurs with the use of progressive technologies is the result.

Despite this increase in the level of poverty, it is fair to comment that Kazakstan retains an advantage in comparison with states such as those in Southeast Asia, because of the high educational and qualificational level of the target group in Kazakstan.

Self-employment is now the primary growth area in employment in Kazakstan. Actual income of the self-employed is differentiated by the type of work and other factors. The majority of the population is engaged in street trading of cheap consumer goods (newspapers, books, tea, gum, etc.). This can earn from T300–400 per week up to T300–400 per day. Such income would not be possible if the trade was done officially (that is, by buying a licence, and paying for a market space). Clothes market space in Almaty is T150–300 per day, and it is T230 per day for the food market. This is in comparison to a seller for a wholesale firm, who for an outlay of T11 800 for 26 working days can expect to turn over T300–1500 per day.

The income from home grown produce sold by the self-employed (at the cottage industry level) can range from T1500 to T10 000 per month. Whilst the minimum income level necessary to stay above the poverty line is not officially established in Kazakstan, USAID defined the minimal consumer basket in Kazakstan as T2900 per month. According to the estimation of the Association of Sociologists and Politologists under the Centre for Euro-Asian Studies (Reading, UK), the consumer basket for defining the poverty line is T6206 per month, including T3208 for food, T1753 for other goods, and T1245 for services. It is thus possible to conclude that self-employment is not only a very difficult and time consuming process, but that the returns from self-employment are unlikely to justify the effort put in.

The process of transition has affected the residential building industry. The amount of new houses built in 1995 (1.2–1.3 million square metres) was one fifth of what it was in 1988. The 1995 figure was in turn 31 per cent less than that of 1994. The situation became particularly difficult in agricultural regions (the relevant difference being 64–70 per cent). The average living space is 15 square metres, compared with the centrally issued norm of 18 square metres (the rural/urban split is 13.5 square metres rural, and 16.3 square metres urban, respectively). There is also evidence of an increase in the economic housing divide, as there is a gradual decrease in state owned houses, and a corresponding increase in construction based upon private investment (which is only available to the most prosperous section of the population).

The final socio-economic factor which should be considered is the very real long-term danger inherent in the ecological problems inherited by Kazakstan. Areas such as the Caspian Sea coast, the Aral Sea, the radioactive danger zones such as Semipaltinsk, Atyrau and Mangystau Oblasts, are either current ecological disaster areas, or are likely to shortly become so. There is a certain immediate necessity to deal with these problems, and there is a definite need to plan ahead in order to prevent the situation deteriorating to the extent that the Kazakstani government risks losing control over events.

In addition, lack of investment and further employment opportunities has been a contributory factor in a marked decline in the state of the Kazakstani intelligentsia and institutions (GDP expenditure on Science has been a constant 0.19 per cent since 1990). Amongst other things, this has led to a brain drain, as leading academics and privileged children leave Kazakstan for education/employment. The education system is in decline across the whole spectrum, with many secondary schools, primary schools and kindergartens closing due to lack of finance.

Kazakstan needs substantial and specific changes in social and public health problems that have accumulated in many crisis areas. All these problems cannot be solved in one day, and it is necessary to implement a whole raft of measures which require systematic performance. This in turn, of course requires a lot of financial resources and coherent and long-term economic and political support.

Conclusion

What is the nature of the transition in Kazakstan? Kazakstan has reconsidered its own system, priorities and future. This has also led to reconsideration of Kazakstan's relationship with neighbours and other countries. The pragmatic concerns of world society and the interdependence of new national economies have led economic systems in differing directions. Certainly the last decade has provided some lessons for Kazakstan, and the next generation will judge in which period the economy of Kazakstan gained the most – before or during transition. This is a concluding chapter, and cannot answer such a complicated question, in fact it is fair to say it is too early to reach conclusions. Nevertheless there are some dimensions which should be emphasised.

BEFORE TRANSITION

Kazakstan was a single part of a unitary economic system – the Soviet economy. During the Soviet era Kazakstan benefited a lot in human development and social conditions, and developed industrial production and infrastructure. In the USSR Kazakstan occupied a leading position in a lot of mining industries, in grain production, etc. The material and industrial base of Kazakstan today is a result of the Soviet period. The Union government made a lot of investments and provided substantial support for the development of the Kazakstani economy.

There were some factors which had a negative influence upon economic development. The most difficult and complicated problem was that Kazakstan was never considered as a separate country, but as an element (republic) of the Union economy. Therefore Kazakstan, according to the Union labour specialisation, had only a few sectors (or even parts of sectors) of the economy which were relatively developed. In addition, of course the whole economic system in Kazakstan was oriented to the USSR's economic interests. At the same time, Kazakstan benefited a lot (in economic terms) from being a part of the USSR. Practically all industries which appeared by 1991 were established during the Soviet period. The popular academic inference that Kazakstan (and other republics) were exploited during the Soviet period both simplifies the issue and is not necessarily correct, as the main target of all economic reforms in the USSR was the creation of a single economic system. In this respect, Kazakstan was only a small part of this system, and the establishment of a 'stand alone' economic system in a small area of the USSR (Kazakstan) would not have been rational. It would indeed be odd if Her Majesty's Government decided to create an autonomous economic system in Wales, or the US government created an autonomous economic system in Texas. No doubt through certain economic discrimination in managerial aspects (including the top governmental level) there were also some obstacles, as the vertical dependence of all organisational bodies in Kazakstan upon Moscow did not allow the creation of Kazakstan's own leaders and an environment which would permit the development of some type of entrepreneurial climate.

TRANSITION

Since the end of 1991 Kazakstan, along with the other newly independent states, has been travelling along the path of economic reforms. In the initial stage of transition the main obstacle for Kazakstan was the issue of understanding what the new country wished to achieve through the socio-economic transformation. The single monetary zone did not allow Kazakstan to conduct its own economic policy until November 1993 (the date of the introduction of the Kazakstani new currency, Tenge). The strong interdependence between CIS countries forced Kazakstan into a position of following the economic reforms initiated by Russia. There is no doubt that the policy of price liberalisation disabled the Kazakstani economic system, and the inflation which immediately arose after the first steps in transformation of prices was an inflation of costs.

At the same time the government of Kazakstan attempted to introduce the plan of reforms called the *Programme of Urgent Anti-Crisis Measures and the Promotion of Socio-Economic Reforms* (1993). It was obvious that the new ruling elite did not have a precise idea regarding the economic future of Kazakstan, as repeatedly one foreign model of development was changed for an alternative model (from a South Korean model to a Turkish model, and from a Turkish model to some sort of *Kazakstani* model).

In 1992 international organisations suggested Kazakstan adopt the package of reforms which had been implemented in Latin America. The main elements of such a package were: a programme of privatisation, price liberalisation, reduction of public expenditure, adjustment of the economic structure, establishment of a new investment climate, liberalisation of foreign trade and on this basis the promotion of open export-oriented economy.

The main mistake here by the Kazakstani government was in focusing on speed as the priority for such reforms. As a result, privatisation, which included several steps (housing privatisation, small and mass privatisation, privatisation through the individual projects) became a purely political (and in some cases corrupted) process. Privatisation as a transformation of social ownership to private property rights simply did not happen, and in addition the attempt at privatisation caused great damage to a lot of Kazakstani industries. In agriculture the collapse of livestock production has damaged the agrarian sector of the economy to such an extent that it will take thirty years to recover.

During the last seven years the Kazakstani government has adopted four anti-crisis programmes. The difficulties with all of them were the unclear economic position taken by the government, and the absence of concrete aims for reform. The negative result of such uncertainty regarding the method of the transformation of the old economic system is that the population does not support the current course of reforms. This lack of confidence was underlined by the increase in the level of poverty, the decline in the standard of living, as well as the behaviour of government officials who did not encourage the recovery of the economy, as in some respects they demonstrated a lack of belief in their own methods (for example the educational programme *Bolashak*, during which the bulk of the children of educational officialdom went overseas for their own education, and in many cases failed to return, prompting a public Presidential response).

All these factors prompted public disappointment and a demand for a return to the previous economic system, because the type of leader (Communist or Democrat) loses importance when personal and family poverty becomes a real possibility.

One of the major problems with the newly independent states (probably excluding Russia) was a lack of managerial personnel to run the transition. In this respect Russia entered into the period of transition with a relative advantage over states such as Kazakstan which had, for example, no experience in the formulation of a foreign economic policy.

No less serious a problem for the Kazakstani economy is the problem of tax collection. At the present time there are a lot of enterprises which remain under inter-enterprise arrears and near bankruptcy, and the Kazakstani economy is dangerously close to a fiscal crisis, resulting from a build-up of payment arrears which are now nearly half the country's GDP. Privatisation is nearly finished, but the result cannot be viewed in a positive light when the share of privatised enterprises is still very low in the Kazakstani GDP. The Kazakstani economy remains in long-term stagnation.

The pessimism of foreign investors regarding business in Kazakstan came through the lack of competence on the part of the government bureaucracy, in particular regarding some industrial objects transferred to the control of the foreign companies and later reclaimed.

The idyllic dream of the government that the oil and gas industries could save Kazakstan from economic collapse is now in the past. The geopolitical situation with regard to pipelines, as well as the lack of refineries, made it difficult to establish oil and gas as the specific source for economic recovery. Kazakstan began an ambitious programme to increase production (and subsequently the export) of oil and gas. This programme necessarily affects the national interests of many countries and multinational companies and cannot be implemented easily. In economic terms, the oil programme is not supported by the financial resources.

Currently it is difficult to see the real possibility for macroeconomics stabilisation. The Kazakstani economy is still in crisis. The decline in output is greater than expected by economists at the start of the Kazakstani economic reforms, when the common opinion was that the recovery was poised to take place.

The following points emerge from the above analysis. The process of transition undergone by Kazakstan (and obviously other socialist countries) since 1991 differs fundamentally from economic re-organisational periods undergone by many countries throughout economic history. This transition means shifting the economic system from one stable state to another. It is not simply a process of creating or modifying a sector or sectors of the economy, indeed it is not even simply an economic operation. The social structure of the post-socialist country is undergoing a profound transformation, based as it was upon the socialist ethos, which pervaded every sector of society. The process of transition is one of extremes. It is impossible to draw guidance from a successful blueprint from the past, and for each nation transition differs, as none follow exactly the same path. It is fair to say that Kazakstan is a typical post-Soviet Central Asian economy and that in the context of the general debate it is possible to say that by 1992 the Kazakstani economy was not ready to adopt the package of reforms suggested by international organisations to all the newly independent states (as well as Central and Eastern Europe). Basically, in the initial stage of transition most newly independent states tried to copy the Polish 'shock therapy' method.

Taken as a whole, the evidence presented in this book suggests that the attempt at shock therapy (in economic terms) by Kazakstan was a mistake, and that a more gradualist approach (both by Kazakstan and the other Central Asian nations) may well have provided stability and greater returns in the long term.

By 1992 the priority for the young country of Kazakstan was the creation of its own national economy. But in the initial euphoria that Kazakstan could now decide all its problems by itself, it is clear that there was not a realistic appraisal of the full dimensions and aspects of independence.

For the initial stage of transition Kazakstan should remain a centrally-planned economy, in other words 'do not destroy the old house without having built a new house'. Kazakstan announced a programme of radical market-orientated reform, an ambitious privatisation programme was initiated, and foreign investment was welcomed, but the lack of competence on the part of government officials simply dropped the whole idea of the reforms. On the one hand, the new economic mechanisms were not constructed, whilst on the other hand the centrally-planned rules were instantly abolished. The economic reforms were accompanied by weak institutional changes. One of the most important mistakes by the Kazakstani government was to neglect the possibility of a dramatic increase in social costs. Large falls in income, unemployment, decreasing of living standards, uncertainty of the future – all these factors adversely affected the confidence of the local population, which could remember the standard of living before transition, and which could not condone the policy of the Kazakstani government bureaucracy (the government still does not know exactly where the country is going) as a route to the new economy. The public mentality in Kazakstan was not ready for a sharp reorientation of human values.

At the present time there are debates regarding the choice of the transitional approach. As Kekic remarks: 'The transition has been characterised by a debate between proponents of either rapid or gradual change about the impact on performance of the pace of transformation' (Kekic, 1996: 12). Gros and Steinherr remain unconvinced that the primary method for reform is shock therapy (Gros and Steinherr, 1995), whilst Balcerowicz is convinced that shock therapy was responsible for the success of the Polish transitional period: '... radical economic reforms, resolutely pursued, were the best choice for bringing about disinflation, structural change, and the takeoff into economic growth and market capitalism.' (Balcerowicz, 1995: 159). On the other hand, there is some advocating of a gradualist approach: '... a progressive way under which rough ideas and principles are determined in advance. And reform is carried out in certain fields with high prospects for success ... reforms are gradually expanded by making the best use of the situation, over a broader area and from grassroot units to the superstructure.' (Shanquan and Fulin, 1995: 7).

From my point of view Kazakstan (and probably other Central Asian countries) could not follow the rapid approach which was successful in some Eastern European countries; '... aspects of the implementation of this policy brought into some disrepute, and changes of ministers in charge of the process added to the problem'. (Kaser, 1997: 27). The main reason for this may be a lack of performance in these countries before transition. In this case the planned interventionist strategy has proven more effective than the more open policies of radical reforms.

The shock therapy approach to some economies of transition is vehemently denounced as bringing 'shock but no therapy' to the economy. Instead, the evolution of Kazakstan into a free-market orientated economy was to be via a consecutive step-by-step evolution.

AFTER TRANSITION (EPILOGUE)

I would like to come back to this book after fifteen years and completely rewrite this conclusion, starting from the point that '... today Kazakstan is one of the most developed countries in the world'. One obstacle to achieving this is the lack of economic rationalism in the policy of government.

But the underlying evils which can cause such detrimental failures and tragedies for Kazakstan (the decline of personal responsibility, the lack of a framework of values for private and public behaviour) are still unclear. Can we stop the negative causation now? There is one very strong resource which Kazakstan had, has and will continue to have. This consists of educated human resources. There is a reason to believe that Kazakstan will be able to move towards economic recovery provided that more appropriate policies are adopted in order to save and develop Kazakstan, and lead Central Asia's largest country into the prosperous and productive twenty-first century it deserves.

Notes

CHAPTER 1   THE KAZAK SOVIET SOCIALIST REPUBLIC IN THE USSR

1. The Virgin Lands Scheme was initiated in 1953 by Khrushchev. The proposal for northern Kazakstan and southern Siberia advocated vast (35 million hectares) areas of grazing land being cultivated, irrigated and planted with wheat.
2. By 'non-rational' refer to an uneven pattern of investment, specifically in this case referring to the lack of 'filter-down' effect from oilfield-specific investment.

CHAPTER 2   THE YEARS OF *PERESTROIKA* IN THE KAZAK SOVIET SOCIALIST REOUBLIC

1. For an analysis of this aspect of the Soviet economy, refer to Kornai, 1992: 180–86 and for an analysis which is connected with small level of substitution capital on real labour, refer to Easterly and Fischer 1992.
2. Note that I am not using the term 'profit', because it is not appropriate for an analysis of a centrally planned system.

CHAPTER 3   THE BEGINNING OF SOVEREIGNTY AND THE END OF THE ROUBLE ZONE

1. Sectoral analysis from Y. Kalyuzhnova, 'The Creation of Structural Policy in the Republic of Kazakstan in the Period of Transition to the Market Economy', unpublished PhD thesis (in Russian).
2. Later in 1994 in the English edition this paragraph was removed from the original Russian text (Nazarbayev, 1994: 24).
3. The main principle of the Kazakstani government was a *strategy of survival*, and the pressure to support production was felt in sectors of the economy.
4. For example, in the Russian version of 'A Strategy for the Development of Kazakstan as a Sovereign State, (Nazarbayev, 1992a) the first stage of development was described as '1992–1995' and in the English version (Nazarbayev, 1994) the first stage of development was described as '1994–1995'. Documents which are presented to the International Financial Organisations in English are not mass distributed and are unknown to the majority of the population.

CHAPTER 4   THE INTRODUCTION OF THE NATIONAL CURRENCY AND THE NEW COURSE OF REFORM

1. Note that by May 1993 both Ukraine and Kyrgyzstan had broken away from the rouble zone, and in the second half of that year Turkmen and Uzbek currencies appeared.
2. It is still a great secret how these credits were implemented.
3. It was a joke at the time that the presence of some of the new 'businessboys' in the corridors of the Presidential Office was a sure sign of forthcoming credits to the country.

CHAPTER 6   STRUCTURAL TRANSFORMATION

1. I omit the detailed analysis of every part because on the one hand all these parts look interesting and promising, but on the other hand it is difficult to predict what kind of consequences the Kazakstani economy will have to suffer from the debt crisis, the calculation of GDP in the 'positive side' and the finished 'elite privatisation' as well as the transfer of all control of enterprises which belong to the export sector of the economy to foreign companies.
2. In the initial stage of the Kazakstani property transformation, this process was called a transfer of enterprises to the jurisdiction of the foreign firms. In reality, such a process cannot be defined as a transfer, because foreign companies took responsibility for repayment of parts of the enterprises' debts, and paid salaries from the financial sources of the foreign firms. All this can be called sales of enterprises.
3. *Karmetkombinat* employs 38 000 workers and has a capacity to produce 6 million tons of steel per year.

CHAPTER 7   BREAKING NEW GROUND

1. How will the definition of Caspian Sea (sea or lake) affect the division of its resources? And how will it affect Kazakstan?
2. *Journal of Comparative Economies*, USA, Vol. 19, December 1994, p. 344.

CHAPTER 8   SECTORS IN TRANSITION

1. Trade data from differing sources has proven inconsistent. For the purposes of this analysis, I have used the data from *Kazakstan Economic Trends*.
2. In particular, suitcase trade reduces pressure for payment of salaries and wage arrears.

3. Importers have increasingly complained that the quality control process is time wasting and unnecessarily expensive.
4. 'The human development index (HDI) measures the levels of three equally weighted primary opportunities for developing human potential: a long and healthy life, access to knowledge, and real gross domestic product (GDP) per capita.' (Kazakstan Human Development Report. 1996: 3).

Bibliography

Akhumbekov, S. (1997), Kanikulu' I 'Krest'yanskii trud' – ponyatiya nesovmes-timue, tem bolee vo vremya reform, *Kazakstanskaya pravda*, 1 March.

Akiner, S. (1995), *The Formation of Kazakh Identity: From Tribe to Nation-state*, London: The Royal Institute of International Affairs.

Amrekulov, N. and Masanov, N. (1994), *Kazakstan Mezhdy Prozhlum I Budushim*, Almaty.

Aslund, A. (1995), How Russia Became a Market Economy. The Brookings Institution, Washington, D.C.

Balcerowicz, L. (1995), *Socialism, Capitalism, Transformation*, Central European University Press, Budapest.

Baumol, W. (1965), *Welfare Economics and the Theory of the State*, London School of Economics London.

Begg, D, and Portes, R. (1992), Enterprise Debt and Economic Transformation: Financial Restructuring of the State Sector in Central and Eastern Europe, CEPR Discussion Paper No. 695.

Buchanan, A. (1985), *Ethics, Efficiency, and the Market*, Clarendon Press, Oxford.

Central Asian Republics: Industrial Development Review. Kazakstan, Kyrgyz Republic and Tajikistan. (1996), Volume I. The Economist Intelligence Unit, United Nations Industrial Development Organisation.

Daviddi, R. and Espa, E. (1995), 'Regional Trade and Foreign Currency Regimes Among the Former Soviet Republics', *Economics Planning*, No. 28, pp. 29–57.

Dittus, P. (1994), Bank Reform and Behavior in Central Europe, in *Journal of Comparative Economics* Volume 19, Number 3, December 1994.

Easterly, W. and Fischer, S. (1995), 'The Soviet Economic Decline', *The World Bank Economic Review*, Vol. 9, No. 3, pp. 341–71.

Economic Commission for Europe (1991), *Economic Survey of Europe in 1990–1991*, New York and Geneva.

Economic Commission for Europe (1992), *Economic Survey of Europe in 1991–1992*, New York and Geneva.

Economic Commission for Europe (1993), *Economic Survey of Europe in 1992–1993*, New York and Geneva.

Economic Commission for Europe (1994), *Economic Survey of Europe in 1993–1994*, New York and Geneva.

Economic Commission for Europe (1995), *Economic Survey of Europe in 1994–1995*, New York and Geneva.

Economic Commission for Europe (1996), *Economic Survey of Europe in 1995–1996*, New York and Geneva.

Economic Commission for Europe (1997), *Economic Survey of Europe in 1996–1997*, New York and Geneva.

Economist Intelligence Unit, (1996–1997), *Kazakstan*, Country Report.

Elliot, G. (1993), 'Kazakhstan, Nazarbayev, Foreign Investment & Oil', *Louisiana Law Review*, Vol. 53, No. 4, pp. 1243–55.

Goskomstat Kaz SSR (1991), *Regionalnui statisticheskii ezhegodnik Kazakstana* (Annual regional statistics of Kazakstan), Alma-Ata.

Goskomstat Kaz SSR (1991), *Statisticheskii ezhegodnik Kazakstana* (Annual statistics of Kazakstan). Alma-Ata.

Goskomstat Republic of Kazakstan (1995), *Regionalnui statisticheskii ezhegodnik Kazakstana* (Annual regional statistics of Kazakstan, 1994) za 1994 god. Alma-Ata.

Goskomstat Republic of Kazakstan (1996), *Kazakstan i drugie gosudarstva* (Kazakstan and other states). Almaty.

Goskomstat Republic of Kazakstan (1996), *Regionalnui statisticheskii ezhegodnik Kazakstana* (Annual regional statistics of Kazakstan). Alma-Ata.

Gregory, P. (1990), *Restructuring the Soviet Economic Bureaucracy*, Cambridge University Press, Cambridge.

Gros, D. and Steinherr, A. (1995), *Winds of Change: Economic Transition in Central and Eastern Europe*, Longman, London and New York.

Ickes, B.W. and Ryterman R. (1992), 'The inter-enterprise arrears crisis in Russia', *Post-Soviet Affairs*, 8, pp. 331–61.

Ickes, B.W. and Ryterman R. (1993), 'Roadblock to Economic Reform: Inter-Enterprise Debt and the Transition to Markets', *Post-Soviet Affairs*, 9, pp. 231–52.

International Monetary Fund (1992), *Economic Review Kazakhstan*, International Monetary Fund, Washington, D.C.

International Monetary Fund (1997), *International Financial Statistics*, International Monetary Fund, February, Washington, D.C.

Kalyuzhnova, Y. (1995/96a), 'The Slovene and Kazakstani Models of Transition,' Discussion Papers in Economics, Series A, Vol. VIII. No. 330, The University of Reading.

Kalyuzhnova, Y. (1995/96b), 'The Privatization of Property in the Republic of Kazakstan', Discussion Papers in Economics, Series A, Vol. VIII. No. 319, The University of Reading.

Kalyuzhnova, Y. and Tucker, N. (1997), 'Geopolitical Factors in Economic Relations: Kazakstani – Russian Relations', *Journal of International Development*, Vol. 9, No. 4, June.

Kalyuzhnova, Y. and Yanovskiy, L. (1995/96a), 'Large-Scale Enterprises Functioning in the Former Soviet Union', Discussion Papers in Quantitative Economics & Computing, Series E, Vol. IV No. 39, The University of Reading.

Kalyuzhnova, Y. and Yanovskiy, L. (1995/96b), 'The Regulation of Monopoly Price in the Kazakstani State Sector', Discussion Papers in Quantitative Economics & Computing, Series E, Vol. IV No. 40, The University of Reading.

Kalyuzhnova, Y. and Yanovskiy, L. (1996/97), 'Analysis of the Economy's Structure in Post – Socialist Countries', Discussion Papers in Quantitative Economics & Computing, Series E, Vol. V No. 44,' The University of Reading.

Kaser, M. (1997), *The Economies of Kazakstan and Uzbekistan*, The Royal Institute of International Affairs. London.

Kazakhstanskaya Pravda (1993), *The Programme of Urgent Anti-Crisis Measures and the Promoting of Socio-Economic Reforms*, 8 April.

Kazakhstanskaya Pravda (1996). March 19, May 13, July 13, August 17, August 20.

Kazakhstanskaya Pravda (1997), *Law about State Support of Direct Investment*, 1 March.

Kazakstan Economic Trends, 1996, First Quarter.

Kazakstan Economic Trends, 1997, January.

Kekic, L. (1996), in Economist Intelligence Unit, (1996), *Economies in transition: Eastern Europe and the former Soviet Union*, Country Forecast, 2nd Quarter 1996.

Kornai, J. (1992), *The Socialist System. The Political Economy of Communism*, Clarendon Press, Oxford.

Koshanov, A., Isaeva, M. and Yesentugelov, A. (eds) (1993), *Economika regiona v usloviyakh perekhoda k runky*, (Economy of the region in the transition to the market), Nasionalnaya Akademiya Nauk Respybliki Kazakstan, Ministerstvo Economiki Respybliki Kazakstan. Almaty.

Kossov, V. and Gurkov, I. (1995), The System of Management in Modern Russia, in *International Studies of Management and Organization*, Vol. 25, No. 4, pp. 9–25.

Kunayev, D. (1992), *O moem Vremeni*. RGZhI 'Daur', MP 'Yntumak', Almaty.

Lavigne, M. (1995), *The Economics of Transition*, Macmillan, London.

Machowski, H. (1985), 'Ost-West Handel: Entwicklung, Interessenlagen, Auschitten', in *Aussenpolitik*, No. 5, s. 5–18, Bonn.

Nasionalno-Statesticheskoe Agenstvo Respublik Kazakhstan (1997), *Social' noeconomicheskoe polozhenie respubliki Kazakhstan za Yanvar-Dekabr' 1996 Goda*, (1997) Goskomstat.

National Bank of Kazakhstan (1996), *Statistical Bulletin*.

Nazarbayev, N. (1992a), 'Strategiya Stanovlenia I Razvitiya Kazakhstana kak Suverennogo Gosudarstva', *Kazakhstanskaya Pravda*, 16 May.

Nazarbayev, N. (1992b), *Without Right and Left*, Class Publishing, London.

Nazarbayev, N. (1994), A Strategy for the Development of Kazakstan as a Sovereign State, The Ministry of Foreign Affairs of the Republic of Kazakhstan, The Embassy of the Republic of Kazakstan, February 14.

Nazarbayev, N. (1994), O sozdanii Evraziiskogo Soyuza, *Kazakhsatnskaya pravda*, 7 June.

Nurushin, E. (1994), 'I respect present government. But I do not care who is sitting in the government', exclusive interview by the president of KRAMDS corporation, Victor Tyo in newspaper, *Express K*, 15 November.

O nalogakh I drugikh obyazatel'nukh platezhakh v byudzhet, (1995), *Ukaz prezidenta Respybliki Kazakhstan, imeyushii cilu zakona*.

Olcott, M.B. (1995), *The Kazakhs*, 2nd Edition, Hoover Institution Press, Stanford, CA.

Operativnaya Svodka Gosudarstvennogo Statisticheskogo Komiteta (1997), January. *Panorama 1996*, N 45.

Orlowski, L. (1995), 'Direct Transfers Between the Former Soviet Union Central Budget and the Republics: Past Evidence and Current Implications', *Economics of Planning*, Vol. 28, pp. 59–73.

Pomfret, R. (1995), *The Economies of Central Asia*, Princeton University Press, Princeton, NJ.

Pomfret, R. (1996), *Asian Economies in Transition: Reforming Centrally Planned Economies*, Edward Elgar, Cheltenham.

Programma neotlozhnukh Antikrizisnukh Mer I Uglubleniya Social'no-Economicheskikh Reform (1993), *Kazakhstanskaya Pravda*, 8 April.

Programme of Government's Activity of Increasing Reforms and Recovery from an Economic Crisis (1994), *Kazakhstanskaya Pravda*, 29 July.

Rumer, B. (ed.) (1996), *Central Asia in Transition: Dilemmas of Political and Economic Development*, Armonk, New York London.

Schattschneider, E. (1960), *The Semi-Sovereign People*, Holt, Rinehart & Winston, New York.

Schumacher, E. (1973), *Small is Beautiful*, Vintage. London.

Selskoe khozya'stvo Respubliki Kazakhstan (1996), Goskomstat Respubliki Kazakhstan.

Shangquan, G. and Chi Fulin (1995), *Theory and Reality of Transition to a Market Economy*, Foreign Languages Press, Beijing.

Social'no-ekonomicheskoe polozhenie respubliki Kazakhstan (1997), *Goskomstat*.

Starr, F. (1997), 'Power Failure. American Policy in the Caspian', *The National Interest*, Spring, 20–31.

Statisticheskii Yezhegodnik Kazakhstana (1991, 1994, 1995) Almaty.

The 1996–98 Action Programme for the Deeping of Reforms 1996–1998.

UNDP (1995), *Kazakstan Human Development Report*, UNDP, Almaty.

UNDP (1996), *Kazakstan Human Development Report*, UNDP, Almaty.

Vneshnyaya torgovlya respubliki Kazakhstan so stranami dalnego zarubezh'ya v 1993 godu (1994), Kazinformszenter, Almaty.

Wieczynski, J. (eds) (1980), *The Modern Encyclopedia of Russian and Soviet History*, Academic International Press, Vol. 16.

World Bank (17 March 1992), *Kazakhstan: The Challenge of Economic Development*, Draft Report prepared by first World Bank mission to Kazakhstan during January 14–24, 1992.

World Investment Report (1996), United Nations, New York and Geneva.

Index